EDITING IN A UNIX™ ENVIRONMENT: THE VI/EX EDITOR

D1429753

Mohamed el Lozy

Prentice-Hall, Inc.
Englewood Cliffs, New Jersey 07632

Business and Professional Book Division

Prentice-Hall International, Inc., *London*
Prentice-Hall of Australia, Pty. Ltd., *Sydney*
Prentice-Hall Canada Inc., *Toronto*
Prentice-Hall of India Private Ltd., *New Delhi*
Prentice-Hall of Japan, Inc., *Tokyo*
Prentice-Hall of Southeast Asia Pte. Ltd., *Singapore*
Whitehall Books, Ltd., *Wellington, New Zealand*
Editora Prentice-Hall do Brasil Ltda., *Rio de Janeiro*
Prentice-Hall Hispanoamericana, S.A., *Mexico*

Editor: George E. Parker

First Printing February 1985

UNIX is a trademark of Bell Laboratories.

Library of Congress Cataloging in Publication Data

el Lozy, Mohamed.
   Editing in a UNIX environment.

   Bibliography: p. 212
   Includes index.
   1. UNIX (Computer operating system) 2. Text editors
(Computer programs) 1. Title.
QA76.6.I69   652'.5   84-22281

ISBN 0-13-235599-X

Printed in the United States of America

The Practical Value
This Book Offers

Of all the tools with which a modern interactive computer comes, the editor is the most used and the one most important for productive work. The original UNIX editor, **ed,** was a sophisticated line-oriented editor, very suitable for the slow terminals that were standard at that time. It has now been largely replaced, for simple text entry and modification, by a powerful screen-oriented editor, **vi,** while the line-oriented component has been upgraded into **ex.**

The price of this added power is increased complexity. Furthermore, the documentation which accompanies **vi/ex** seems to be directed to the experienced computer user, and is not really suitable for those whose first contact with computers is through **vi/ex.** Until now, the alternative has been the brief handouts given out by most computer centers. They are adequate for getting started but do not begin to explore the full possibilities of the editor. As a result, many users do not take full advantage of the capabilities of this truly outstanding tool.

This book will help to make the task of learning **vi/ex** easier. I will cover all that a user will need to know about it, starting slowly and adding functions gradually. The beginner will be able to do some simple editing after reading the first two chapters, and even the most experienced users will find something new.

As noted above, the editor can be used in two modes; a reasonably easy-to-use visual mode (**vi**) for text entry and modification, and a more sophisticated line-oriented one (**ex**) used for complex file rearrangements. The line-oriented commands are always available in the visual mode. The three parts of the book travel along the path of increasing sophistication, from purely visual editing (Part I) to the use of **ex** commands in the visual mode (Part II) and ending with the stand-alone use of the **ex** component (Part III).

Parts I and II cover everything needed to do any task for which the visual mode is appropriate. For some readers this may be sufficient, though I hope that all will at least dip into Part III. Part III covers the line-oriented aspects of the editor, with special emphasis on the use of editor scripts to make systematic changes in structured files. It also briefly covers the stand-alone use of **ex** on slow or printing terminals. The final chapter describes other useful editing tools available in the UNIX environment, justifying the generality of the first part of the book's title.

Chapter 1 is a brief introduction to the terminal. Its main purpose is to establish the terminology used in the rest of the book, not to instruct the novice in the use of the terminal and the system in general. I feel that the best way to get started is to ask a more experienced user for help.[1] Chapter 2 is a brief introduction to **vi** that can be covered easily in one session at the terminal. It will help you to do some basic editing while going through the next three chapters.

Chapters 3 to 5 discuss fully most of the screen-related commands of the editor. Chapter 3 deals with text entry. You will be asked to enter a small file, containing part of the Declaration of Independence, both as an exercise in text entry and as a source of examples in the following chapters. Chapter 4 describes the commands that allow you to move around the file you are editing,

---

[1]An excellent introductory book on UNIX is *A UNIX Primer* by Lomouto and Lomouto, Prentice-Hall, Inc., 1983. It contains a very good step-by-step introduction to the **ed** editor, but nothing on the **vi** editor.

while Chap. 5 completes this part with a description of the commands for adding, changing, and moving text.

Part II deals with the line-oriented commands that are important to those using the editor primarily in its visual mode. Chapter 6 describes the most important options that the user can set; while they affect the operations in visual mode they are set in the line-oriented mode. Chapter 7 covers the file-oriented commands, together with the relevant options. Chapter 8 ends Part II with a discussion of several line-oriented commands that can be very useful in the visual mode.

Part III deals mostly with **ex**, the line-oriented part of the editor. It begins with Chap. 9, which describes all the **ex** commands that have not been described earlier. Chapter 10 then describes what I call the "magic ingredients" of **ex**: the pattern-matching ability, the substitute command, and the global commands. The main purpose of these two chapters is to enable you to write editor scripts (Chap. 11), which are really programs that can be used to make systematic changes in files. These are most useful in structured files, but also have a variety of other uses. The book ends with Chap. 12, in which several important UNIX tools for file manipulation are described.

A series of Appendixes give the various **vi** and **ex** commands and options, the command line syntax of the editor commands, and finally an annotated reading list.

VERSIONS

The increasing number of UNIX versions should not be a problem for readers of this book, as the differences between versions have little effect on the editor. This book was written using the Berkeley release version 4.2, but almost all the material will apply to any UNIX system that can run **vi** or **ex**. The very few commands that apply only to Berkeley versions will be noted as they arise.

Potentially more troublesome are differences between versions of the editors. This book used version 3.6 of **ex**, which is a fully developed product to which major changes are not anticipated. On the other hand, it does differ from version 2 and its derivatives, which are found in some microcomputer adaptations of the UNIX system. Those few commands that are not found on all currently available versions will be noted as they arise. Users of the earlier version should consult their reference manuals to see exactly what is implemented on their system.

Appendix E discusses the differences between versions in some detail, and describes the editor available on one particular microcomputer implementation.

Mohamed el Lozy

Acknowledgments

This book was written on the UNIX system which has made all aspects of computing much more pleasant for me for several years. It was introduced in our Health Sciences Computing Facility by its then Director, Dr. Raymond Neff (now Director of Academic Computing at Dartmouth), who urged me to switch from OS/MVS. I received much help over the years from a succession of systems programmers, and especially want to thank Jeremy Pool (now at Bolt, Beranak, and Newman), Don Olivier, Ken Chin and Neil Rhodes.

My thanks to Stephen D. Dragin, Electronics Product Manager for the Professional Books Division at Prentice-Hall, for his enthusiastic support for this book. I must also thank an unfortunately anonymous reviewer whose pithy comments certainly improved the book.

CONTENTS

GETTING STARTED

This book assumes that you know little or nothing about computers, UNIX, or editing, and that you need to use all three of them for programming, text processing, or whatever other reason you may have. If you are a more experienced user moving from another system, or a UNIX user making the switch from **ed**, please be patient and remember that you were once a beginner yourself!

An editor, sometimes called a text editor, is a program that is used to enter material into the computer. That material is likely to be either a program that will be compiled and run later or continuous text that will be printed out; I will use the term text to refer to either.

Why is an editor required? After all, home computers can run BASIC programs without using an editor, and many word processing systems have their own built-in editor. The reason for a separate editor is at the heart of the UNIX philosophy: It is better to have several tools, each of which does one job, and does it well, than to have a smaller number of tools, each of which does many things, often not too well. Furthermore, what about a person who writes programs and then has to write reports on their results? In a home computer system that person would have to learn how to enter and modify programs using BASIC's way of doing it, then learn a different system for entering and modifying the text for the report. In the UNIX scheme of things a single editor does both.

The **vi/ex** editor that we will be studying was developed at the University of California at Berkeley, where many improvements were made to the basic UNIX system originally developed at Bell Laboratories. It is probably one of the most important of the Berkeley additions, and is now standard on both the Bell Laboratories and Berkeley versions of UNIX. It is also included with most of the UNIX-like systems running on microcomputers. As its name indicates, it has two components, a visually oriented **vi** and a line oriented **ex**.

The **vi** component that we will study in Part I is a screen-oriented editor, which means that the screen shows you part of the text you are editing. We often refer to the screen as being a window on the text. You can move that window over your text, and you can move within that window. Specifically you can add or remove text within that window. Note that changing text means removing the old text and adding new text, so this is not a separate type of activity, though it is sometimes convenient to treat it as such. Finally you can save your text so that it will be there when you need it at some later time.

Adding text, removing it, moving around it and finally saving it; that is all there is to editing. Then why a whole book on the subject? The editor we will be describing is a powerful one that can do many things that simpler ones cannot. These things make life much easier for the user once they have been learned, but take some time to learn.

This is a book about the editor, not about the UNIX system. You will have to learn how to use the system from some other source. While most computing centers have some handouts for beginners, the best way to get started is with the help of another user. Once you are started you should learn as much about the system as you can. The first thing to read is probably Brian W. Kernighan's section entitled "UNIX for Beginners" in the *UNIX Programmer's Manual.* Appendix F gives more detail about this publication and describes some books that are available, should you wish to learn more.

For best results Part I at least should be read sitting at a terminal, trying out each new command and generally experimenting with the editor. While it will take time, the objective is to reach a stage in which your fingers do the editing for you. You decide what you want your text to be, and your fingers will do what needs to be done. This can only be attained through practice. In any case, enjoy yourself! The editor is a remarkably responsive tool, and I hope you will agree with me that using it is fun.

NOTE FOR ED USERS

You have an obvious advantage over newcomers to the UNIX system in that you are familiar with the environment. You may further believe that the similarities between **ed** and the **vi/ex** editor will help you get started. In fact, the contrary is true. A display-oriented editor is fundamentally different from a line-oriented one, and you will need to learn the fundamentals in Chapters 2 to 5 from scratch. Your previous knowledge will bear fruit in Parts II and III, where you will discover that the **ex** editor is very similar to **ed** though there are some differences (mainly enhancements added to **ex**).

Initially you may well be tempted to escape from **vi** to the underlying **ex** editor; resist this temptation. This is very much like learning to touch type after years spent typing with two fingers; initially using two fingers is faster, but the only way to become a fast typist is to stop two-fingered typing. I have used this example because I believe that the difference between **vi** and **ed** is as great as the difference between touch typing and the two-fingered approach.

1

Communicating with Your Computer

Getting started involves learning something about UNIX in general, and about how it is implemented in your installation. Installations differ considerably in the details of how things are done; most have some kind of handout material for beginners. In any case, the fastest way to get started is to ask someone who knows. In addition, you will have to learn how to communicate with your computer, both in general and in relation to **vi**.

There are now two common kinds of computing installations running UNIX and the **vi/ex** editor. The first is the more traditional multiuser system in which several users are connected separately to a computer, with each user accessing the computer through a terminal that is not part of the computer itself. A more recent development has been single-user systems that run some derivative of UNIX, almost always with a different name. In these systems there is no separate terminal, as the user interface is built into the computer.

In either case the user communicates with the computer via a keyboard and screen combination; the keyboard sends information from the user to the computer, and the screen shows information from the computer. There is little need to distinguish between these two situations, and I will use the word "terminal" to refer to the keyboard and screen, whether they are packaged as a separate terminal or are part of the computer.

1.1 THE STANDARD KEYBOARD

Both terminals and stand-alone computers have keyboards similar to those of typewriters, but with additional keys. Standard keyboards are capable of sending 128 different characters to the computer.[1] These include the alphabet in both cases, numbers, and numerous special symbols. In addition, 32 different control characters (item 2 below) can be sent. Users of the **vi** editor should specially note the following keys:

1. **Return, enter, newline,** or something similar. It is usually larger than the other keys and may be of a different color and plays the same role as the carriage return key of an electrical typewriter. We will refer to it as **CR**. As a general rule the computer will not begin to process your instructions till you press that key. Unfortunately **vi** is an exception to that rule, with many instructions that take effect immediately, without your hitting **CR**; this may cause some initial confusion.

   On some terminals you may have two keys, one labeled **return** and the other **newline**. Ask an experienced user which you should use.

2. **Control.** This is like a second shift key and is used to generate extra instructions to the computer. Like the shift key, you hold the **control** key down while depressing a character key. The result of that combination is referred to as **Control–X**, where X is the character pressed. The **vi** editor uses the control characters extensively to enter instructions.

   As noted above, there are 32 control codes, but there are only 26 letters. The location of the other six control characters is variable. If you ever need to know how to send a control character not associated with a letter you will have to look it up in the manual (or ask someone who knows).

3. **Delete or rubout.** This is used by some systems to send a signal to the computer (interrupt) to cancel whatever it is doing. Other systems use **Control–C** for that purpose, and on these systems delete is often used to erase the last character entered (erase key). We will refer to the interrupt key (whatever character it is) as **INT**.

4. **Escape.** This is usually found at the left side of the keyboard and may be labeled **ALT**. It plays an essential role in **vi** and *must* be identified before starting to use that editor. We will refer to it as **ESC**.

5. **Tab**. This acts like the tab key on a typewriter. Normally the tab stops are automatically set at positions that are multiples of eight. Tabs are used extensively in preparing tables and in indenting programs. **Control–I** has the same effect as tab.

6. Other keys often found are a **break** key, which often sends a special kind of interrupt to the system, and a **linefeed** key, which may be different in function from the return key.

7. Finally, you will find a variety of characters that are not found on an ordinary typewriter. They include backslash, "\," reverse single quote, " `," tilde, "~," braces, "{," "}," brackets, "[," "]," and the vertical bar "|," known as the "pipe" symbol, which plays a large role in the UNIX system.

It is important to know which keys do what on the system that you are using. An excellent rule while getting started is: when in doubt, ask.

When entering text you will obviously make errors. Every computer has two or three keys that will allow you to remove the erroneous entries. One key, referred to as the **erase** character, deletes just the last character entered. Pressing it twice will delete the last two characters, and so on until you reach the start of the line (it will not delete text on previous lines). A second key, referred to as the **kill** character, will delete all you have entered on the current line.

In the past these keys were often **#** for erase and **@** for kill. Many installations today use either the **backspace**[2], the **delete**, or the **rubout** key as the erase character, and **Control–U** as the kill character. You may also find that the **Control–W** key will erase the whole of the last word entered; if available, it does save some time.

1.2 OTHER KEYS

In addition to the basic keys that transmit the American Standard Code for Information Interchange (ASCII) codes, many terminals have other keys that may occasionally have unforeseen effects. Almost all have a capital lock key, and in almost every case it works just with letters. To produce the symbol on a number key, for example, you must press the shift key even if the capital lock is on. Furthermore, pressing the shift key will not undo the capital lock; you must press it again to release it. If you log onto the computer with it on, the computer will believe that your terminal is incapable of sending lower case, and will interpret your input in a strange way. Log off, release the capital lock, and log on again.

A very dangerous key found on some terminals is a **no scroll** key. Pressing it will interrupt all communications between your terminal and the computer, while pressing it a second time will restore them. On most systems **Control–S** will stop communications, while **Control–Q** will restore them.

Here again, the cardinal rule is to ask someone who knows. If you are going to use a certain type of terminal regularly, find out which keys can get you into trouble and, more to the point, what to do if you press them.

1.3 OTHER FEATURES

Many modern "smart" terminals have a variety of features that are often very useful. Once you know how to do the simplest things with your terminal, it may be useful to read its instruction manual to see what else it can do for you.

One of the most useful of these features is **keyboard repeat**, called typamatic action by some manufacturers. On a Digital Equipment Corporation VT100 terminal it works as follows: When a key is typed, its code is sent immediately to the computer, once. If the key is held down for more than half a second, the code repeatedly will be sent to the computer at a rate of approximately 30 times per second until the key is released. If the terminal is transmitting at a low rate, the repetition will be slower. Find out whether your terminal has this feature. It is sometimes quite useful.

In addition, many terminals have function keys that usually send, at a single keystroke, a series of characters to the computer. They can often be used to shorten editing commands (Chap. 8).

NOTES TO CHAPTER 1

1. This standard is often referred to as ASCII, for American Standard Code for Information Interchange. It is universally used on UNIX systems, as well as most other non-IBM ones.

2. **Control–H** has the same effect as **backspace** in all contexts.

2

Getting
to Know vi

The **vi** editor seems to be a complex program as it has options that will allow it to do a great many things. In fact, it is fairly simple to use, as the commands have a regular structure. In this chapter you will learn how to do a few simple things; the following chapters will explore the many additional things it can do. There you will find that many of these more advanced features are extensions of what you have learned here. Thus in this chapter you will learn how to delete single characters or words, and in Chap. 5 you will see that deleting lines, sentences, paragraphs, or parts of them is very similar.

2.1 EDITING MODES

Mode is a concept that can be confusing if not grasped from the start. The editing process consists of two phases: first text is entered, then it is modified. The editor has two corresponding modes: a text insertion mode in which what you enter at the keyboard is taken as text and put in your file, and a command mode in which what you enter is taken as commands to the editor to do various things. Commands exist for moving from one part of your document to another, deleting text or changing to the text insertion mode.

Several commands will put you into the text insertion mode. Entering **ESC**[1] will get you back to command mode. That is why the **ESC** key has to be clearly identified before starting to use **vi**. Once out of text insertion mode, entering **ESC** one or more times will have no effect other than to sound the bell that is in most terminals. When in doubt as to what mode you are in, hit **ESC** a couple of times. It will get you out of insertion mode and ring the bell to reassure you that you are indeed back in command mode.

The only way to learn how to use an editor is to use it, so let us start by writing and modifying a file. Before doing this you must log on and tell the system what type of terminal you are using; ask someone what to do to get started or read your manual.[2]

2.2 ENTERING TEXT

Now let us enter and modify a file called, appropriately enough at this stage, **junk**. To do so type:

vi junk

The screen will be blanked and you will get a message on the bottom line. That message may[3] read

junk, no such file or directory

Don't worry, there is no such file yet, but you are about to create one. Alternately, it may read

junk [New file]

You will notice that many of the lines of the screen are blank except for a "twiddle" at the leftmost margin; these are the lines that you are going to fill with text. That twiddle, incidentally, is called a tilde. You will also notice, at the upper left-hand corner, a blinking symbol, probably an underline but perhaps a solid block. That symbol is called the cursor, and it shows you where, in the text being edited, the computer thinks that you are.

You need some text in the file before you can do any useful editing, so let's enter text insertion mode. The simplest way is to type the letter **i**, *not* followed by a carriage return.[4] Nothing appears on the screen, but you are now in text insertion mode and everything that you enter on the keyboard will appear in your file.

Now type in the following lines, mistakes and all:

Now iss the for
most good man to
come come to the ad
of their parti.

Do not try to correct any other errors you make during text entry at this stage. You will see later how to make corrections during text entry. Type a carriage return at the end of the first three lines, but not at the end of the fourth. After typing the period that ends the sentence enter **ESC**. You will be back in command mode, where the computer will interpret what you type as instructions, not as text to be entered.

2.2.1 WARNING: Trapped in Insertion Mode

It is very frustrating to try and give commands to the editor while you are in insertion mode but do not realize it. You give a command and nothing happens. You try another one, and still no luck. You panic and decide to quit, so you give a **ZZ** or **:q** (Sec. 2.5) command, and still nothing happens!

If you look carefully at your screen you will see the commands you have given in the middle of your text. Remember that while you are in insertion mode *everything* you enter (except **ESC** or **INT**) is taken as text to be entered into your file. So enter **ESC** and delete the "commands" from your file. Do not think that it will not happen to you: if this is the first editor that you use it will!

2.3 MOVING AROUND THE SCREEN

To correct the many errors in the file you have just created you must be able to do three things: move to the location of the error, remove a character that should not be there, and insert a missing character. The ability to remove or insert more than one character at a time will make the editor much more convenient.

There are many ways to move about the screen. Many terminals have four arrow keys, pointing up, down, left, and right. Pressing them will move your cursor one position in the direction the arrow indicates. While they are the most obvious way of moving, I hope that you will not use them, as your fingers will have to leave the conventional keyboard to get to them; this always slows things down.

To move to the right you should use the space bar, which is the same way you move with a typewriter. To move in the other three directions use the **h**, **j**, and **k** keys. The **h** key will move you to the left, the **j** key down, and the **k** key up (the next key, **l**, will move you to the right, but the space bar is more convenient). How do you remember these hopelessly nonmnemonic keys? Of these three keys, **h** is the leftmost, hence it moves to the left[5], **j** goes below the line, hence it moves down, and **k** is the last one. In any case, you will be using them so much that you will have no difficulty in remembering them!

Use these four keys to move around your text. What happens if you try to move to the right when you are at the end of a line, or to the left when you are at the beginning of one? Find out for yourself! You will note two things: first, the cursor does not move off the line it is on, and second, the bell that is in the terminal will ring. The ringing of the bell always means that you have attempted to do something that should not be done. It may, as in this case, be something totally harmless; on the other hand, it may be something more serious. In any case, whenever you hear the terminal "beep" at you, find out what is bothering the editor and, if needed, take corrective action.

2.4 MAKING CORRECTIONS

Now move to the first line (up three times with the **k** key) and position the cursor over the first "s" of "iss." You want to remove that single character. While there are other ways of doing it, the easiest is to enter the single letter command (remember, you are now in the command mode) **x**, which will "x it out," as a careless typist might do.

Note that the **x** does not appear on the screen. As a general rule, **vi** commands do not appear on the screen, and all that you see is their effect. If you absent-mindedly get into a mess you will not be able to see the sequence of commands that got you there.

The cursor will now be over the remaining "s" of the now correct "is." Remove it by hitting **x** again. Why did I ask you to make a mistake? To show you how easy it is to correct an error if you detect it immediately. Try hitting **u** now. It will undo the last (wrong) command and the second "s" deleted will reappear in its place. Try **u** a second time. The effect of the first **u** will be undone, and the "s" will disappear. A third **u** will bring the "s" back. Successive **u** commands will undo each other's effect.

The undo command is one of the most important commands in **vi**. As long as you are looking at the screen and following the effect of each command, it will allow you to recover from any error. Not only that, but it will also give you the freedom to try out things that are not clear. What will happen if I do...? Try it out; if you are dissatisfied with the result, **u** will undo its effect.

This is very important: the only way to learn about computers is to try things out. And the only way to try things out is to have a safety net that will get you out of trouble if what you try does not work. Undo is a safety net; use it to experiment freely with **vi**.

Now back to correcting your file. On line two you have entered "man" instead of "men." You want to replace a single letter by another, and to do that you have the command **r**. Move the cursor over the offending letter and enter in succession the letters "r" (the replace command) and "e" (the replacement letter; no carriage return). The "a" will be changed into an "e," and you will remain in command mode.

The two commands, **x,** and **r,** act on individual characters only. Two similar commands have much greater scope. The command **d** will delete objects, which may be characters, words, lines, sentences, etc. Hence it must be told what kind of object to delete. To try it out, move the cursor to the start of the first of the two repetitions of "come" on line three. Enter **d**, and nothing will happen. The computer is waiting for you to tell it what kind of object to delete. Now enter a space, and you will observe that the "c" has been deleted. The command **d** followed by a space will delete a single character, requiring two keystrokes to do what **x** can do with one. Now undo this with **u** and you should once again have the word "come" twice at the start of the line. This time enter **d** followed by **w** (for word). The whole word will be deleted, as will the space following it. Enter **dd** and the whole line will be deleted. You can restore it, of course, with a **u** command.

Change (abbreviated to **c**) combines the functions of delete and insert, in that it first deletes text and then automatically puts you into insertion mode. Move the cursor to the first letter of the word "most" on line two, and change it to "all." Enter **c** followed by **w** (change word). You will note that the last letter of "most" has been replaced by a $ sign. Everything from where the cursor is to that $ will be replaced by what you now enter. Enter "all" followed by **ESC** (the command **c** put you in text insertion mode and you must get out of it after having entered your text). The $ will disappear, and you will have "all good...." Now move to the "i" at the end of "parti." The easiest way to replace it would be by using **r**, but let's use **c** instead. Enter "c" and follow it by a space to tell the editor that you want to replace a character. The i will be replaced by $, and you should now enter "y" followed by **ESC**. This example was only given to emphasize the similarity between the **c** and **d** commands, since **r** is clearly simpler for changing single characters.

Now for something a little more confusing (perhaps). Move up to the end of line three, where you have "ad" instead of "aid." Move the cursor over the final "d" and enter **i**, to put you in the text entry mode. If you now enter a second "i" you would expect it to be entered before the "d." Instead, the "d" may be overwritten by the "i." Now enter **ESC**, and the "d" should reappear. You will see later that to save computing, the screen may not be updated to reflect changes immediately.

Now move back up to line one, where the word "time" is missing ("Now is the time …"). Move the cursor to the space before "for" and instead of entering **i** (for insert) enter **a** (for append). What you will now enter will be put in the file after the position of the cursor. Enter "time" followed by a space and then **ESC**. The word "for" may well appear to have been overwritten during the addition of "time." It will reappear after the addition is completed.

Append and insert are a pair of very similar commands, which in most cases can be used interchangeably (by putting the cursor in the right position). I tend to use insert most of the time, using append only to add material to the end of a word or line.

2.5 SAVING TEXT AND QUITTING

Before ending the session another important concept must be introduced, and that is the buffer. Text entered into the computer during the editing session is stored in a temporary storage area (often called the buffer) that will be lost after the end of the session. It will not be put into permanent storage unless you so instruct the editor.

The editor will complain if you try and exit it without having saved the file, but it will not save it for you. Try to quit by entering **:qCR**. You will note that the colon appears on the bottom line, and that you must terminate the command with a **CR**; this is an **ex** command (see Chap. 9). The editor will give you a message on that line:

No write since last change (:quit! overrides)

In almost all cases you will want to save your changes. The **:q!CR** command is for those cases in which you have completely messed up your file and you don't want this editing session applied to your file in permanent storage.

This file is not really worth saving, but let's do so anyway. Enter **ZZ** (two upper case Z's) and you will get a line at the bottom of the screen that reads

"junk" [New file] 4 lines, 68 characters.

On the next line you will get the UNIX prompt. If you now give the command

ls

you will get a list of the files in your directory which should include a file called "junk." Now entering

cat junk

should cause the contents of that file to be printed on your terminal.

An explanation of this last command may be called for: cat is a command which will cause the contents of a file to be displayed on the terminal. Is there *any* reasonable explanation for giving the command such a strange name? Yes, but it is not very convincing for the beginner. The program that displays files on the terminal can do many other things; specifically, it can take a series of files and write them all into a common file. This process is called *catenation* (catenate: to connect in a series of ties or links; form into a chain), and is most conveniently abbreviated as "cat." This is a clear example of the kind of logic behind the names of many of the UNIX commands. The UNIX system has much that is excellent in it; you have no choice but to accept the quirks of those who developed it!

2.6 SUMMARY OF COMMANDS

Let us summarize the commands that we have learned in this chapter. The following list gives them and the section in which each was introduced. Note that some commands (**d** and **c**) require an argument (type of object they act on). Note also that the first two commands start with a colon; they are, as noted in the text, **ex** commands.

:q!	quit editor without saving changes (2.5)
:q	quit editor (2.5)
ESC	return to command mode from insertion mode (2.1)

ZZ	save file and quit (2.5)
a	append text (2.4)
c	change object (2.4)
d	delete object (2.4)
h	move left one space (2.3)
i	insert text (2.2)
j	move down one line (2.3)
k	move up one line (2.3)
l	move right one space (**space** is better) (2.3)
r	replace character (2.4)
space	move right one space (2.3)
u	undo last change (2.4)
x	remove character (2.4)

NOTES TO CHAPTER 2

1. Remember, **ESC** refers to the key labeled **ESCAPE**, **ESC** or **ALT** on your terminal, not to the three letter sequence E, S, C. Let's note for the sake of completeness that the interrupt character (**INT**, see Chap. 1) will have the same effect. However, it is much easier if you remember only one of a set of commands which have exactly the same effect.

2. If all else fails, read Sec. 6.2. However, do try to find someone knowledgeable; such a person is almost essential if you have little computing experience.

3. You will notice that I use the word "may" quite often. The reason is that different installations configure the editor in different ways. This will rarely cause a problem, as many of these differences are cosmetic. In most cases the installation has to choose one of several alternative settings for a parameter as the default; if you do not like it you can change it. Chapter 6 will describe these alternatives and make some suggestions.

4. Entering a carriage return after the **i** would enter a blank line before whatever text you then enter.

5. More sophisticated users will remember that **Control–H** generates a backspace.

3

Entering Text

In Chap. 2 you entered a small amount of text, not worrying about how to correct errors during entry. As the first stage in the more detailed study of the editor you will now learn about the various modes of text entry, and how to correct errors during entry. I will attempt to show you efficient ways of doing things, rather than merely teaching you the rules.

3.1 CORRECTING ERRORS DURING INSERTION

Before you get started, let me remind you of the discussion in Chap. 1 of the **erase** and **kill** characters. Each installation chooses what keys to use for these two functions.[1] The **erase** character will, while at the UNIX system level, erase the previous character (if it is on the same line, i.e., if you are not at the start of a line), while the **kill** character will delete all of the current line. You *must* find out what these characters are before going any further.

In the previous chapter you learned the fundamental fact about insertion mode: everything you enter becomes part of the text. It appears on the screen as it is being entered, and during insertions may appear to overwrite the pre–existing text. Though you will not use them in your example, tabs may be inserted using the tab key, as with a typewriter.

Corrections during insertion mode are easy, though at first sight a bit confusing. To erase the last character entered use your normal erase character (Chap. 1).[2] On most systems it will merely backspace over the last character entered, leaving that character on the screen. Don't worry, that character has been erased from the computer's internal representation of your file. When you leave the insertion mode by hitting **ESC**, the screen will be updated to reflect the internal representation. Your kill character will erase (internally, just as erase does) all of your current insertion on the current line (i.e., it will not kill pre-existing text on the line). Finally, **Control–W** will erase the last word entered, leaving you after the space at the end of the previous word.

Note that while you are in insertion mode you can only make changes on the line you are currently entering; if you suddenly notice an error on a previous line, you cannot get to it. That is no real problem, since you can get out of insertion mode and fix it.[3]

3.2 A PRACTICAL EXAMPLE

In the previous chapter you have entered a small amount of text to get a "feel" for editing. Now use your newly acquired knowledge to enter a larger body of text, correcting any errors as you go. This text will be used in almost all the examples in this book. Try and enter it exactly as it is shown; it will be much easier to follow the examples.[4]

The material is part of the Declaration of Independence, so call the file you will put it into "decl." Enter the text in installments to see how various text entry commands can be used. The lines are purposely short so that many lines (37 in fact) of text can be entered with an acceptable amount of work.

Give the command **vi decl** to get started. You will get a message stating either that there is no such file, or that it is a new file. Now enter **i** to get into text entry or insertion mode, and start entering the first paragraph *without* the blanks at the start of the first line or the heading (you will put them in later). Remember *not* to give a **CR** after the initial **i**.

IN CONGRESS, July 4, 1776

THE UNANIMOUS DECLARATION of the thirteen united STATES OF AMERICA

WHEN in the Course of human events it becomes necessary for one people to dissolve the political bands which have connected them with another, and to assume among the powers of the earth, the separate and equal station to which the laws of Nature and Nature's God entitle them, a decent respect to the opinions of mankind requires that they should declare the causes which impel them to the separation.

We hold these truths to be selfevident, that all men are created equal, that they are endowed by their creator with certain unalienable rights, that among these are Life, Liberty and the pursuit of Happiness. That to secure these rights, Governments are instituted among men, deriving their just powers from the consent of the governed. That whenever any Form of Government becomes destructive of these ends, it is the right of the People to alter or abolish it, and to institute new Government, laying its foundation on such principles and organizing its powers in such form, as to them shall seem most likely to effect their Safety and Happiness.

Prudence, indeed, will dictate that Governments long established should not be changed for light and transient causes; and accordingly all experience has shewn that mankind are more disposed to suffer, while evils are sufferable, than to right themselves by abolishing the forms to which they are accustomed.

Fig. 3–1: File Used in Most Examples.

After all these general instructions, let us start. Make some specific errors so that you can learn exactly what happens during the correction process. Begin by entering

"When in"

(first word not in capitals). To back up and correct the errors (sacrificing the correct word "in" in the process), first enter **Control–W**. The cursor will now be under the "i" of "in" with that word still on the screen. Now use your **erase** character to remove the blank and the last three letters of "When," leaving the correct capitalized first letter. The lower case letters are still on the screen, as is the word "in," but you know that they are gone from the computer's representation of your text. Now enter the correct text "WHEN in" and continue that line, ending it with a **CR**.

As you remember, the **h** key will move the cursor to the left while in command mode. What will happen if you use it, rather than the **erase** character, to delete errors during text entry? If you think for a few seconds, the answer should be clear; however, try it (the only proof that your answer is correct is if what you predicted does indeed happen!). While entering the second line omit the space between the words "for" and "one." Now try to backspace over the "one" using the **h** key. What do you get? You will have entered one **h** or more into your text. Are you surprised? You should not be, as you have already entered that letter on the previous line. If **h** had any control effects (such as backspacing) in the text insertion mode, you could never enter it into your text. Hence none of the "ordinary" characters of the keyboard have any special effect in the insertion mode. This is a very important point to grasp.

After you have entered the paragraph, your cursor will be under the period following the last word (separation). Get out of insertion mode and correct any errors you missed while entering text using the methods described in Chap. 2. If a word is badly misspelled it is easier to correct the whole word with **cw** (change word, as you surely remember) than to delete wrong letters and insert missing ones. The different ways of correcting text will be discussed later. Right now you want to get the text in.

A pair of very useful commands (that really belong to the next chapter) work only while you are in the command (as opposed to text insertion) mode. Enter **−**; your cursor should now be at the start of the previous line of text, unless you were already on the first line. Note that this is different from the **k** key, which will move the cursor up one line staying in the same column. **CR** will have the opposite effect; it will move the cursor to the start of the next line. What happens if you give a **CR** when you are at the bottom of the file? Find out by getting to the bottom line with repeated **CRs** and giving one more! You will hear the terminal's electronic bell, which is universally referred to as a "beep." It is a sound that will become very familiar to you as you use **vi**; it means that you have done something wrong (in this case told the cursor to go down when there is no place to go!).

You now want to enter the missing blanks at the start of the first line. Get there by using as many — commands as you need. One way to insert the blanks would be to give an ordinary **i** command. To introduce yourself to a modified insert command, move a few spaces from the start of the line using the space bar. To be specific, get to the end of the second word, "in." Now give the command **I** (capital I). This command will move the cursor to the start of the current line and put you into insertion mode. Follow it by three spaces, and you will probably (it depends on your terminal) find that the letters WHE have disappeared. Now enter **ESC** and they will reappear.

There is a corresponding **A** command that will append to the end of the line; it is in fact used more often than the **I** command. Its use will be demonstrated shortly.

You may not want to enter all the text in one sitting. You will now see how to end an editing session and resume it later. The command **ZZ** will write out your file and return you to the UNIX command level. When you want to resume editing your file, give the command **vi decl** just as you did to create it. The only difference now is that instead of a blank screen you will have part of your text visible on the screen[5], with the cursor under the first character of the first line. Furthermore, you get a message on the bottom line giving the name of the file and the number of lines and characters in it.

.3 A SECOND SESSION

You now want to add the header. You can insert the material before the first blank on what is now the first line. However, this is not really what you want to do. You do not want to insert text on that line, but above it. The proper command is **O** (upper case O) which will insert a line before (above) the line the cursor is on.

Enter the first line, followed by a **CR**, then give a second **CR** to get the blank line. On the third line, leave out the "U" at the beginning of "UNANIMOUS" and continue entering text till the end of the word "the." Assume that you just noted the error at that point and decided to correct it immediately. You could, of course, delete all you had entered after the error, but why delete several perfectly correct words for a single error? Far better to get out of insertion mode, correct the error, and get back into insertion mode.

Hit **ESC** to get out of insertion mode, and move back (with the **h** key) till your cursor is under the "N," then give the sequence of commands **iUESC**; this will insert the missing letter and put you back in command mode. You now want to resume inserting text at the end of the current line. Do you see what the **A** command will do? It will take you from where you are to the end of the line and put you into insertion mode so that you can continue entering text. It is an extremely useful command. It has another common use: adding missing semicolons to the ends of lines of programs written in C, Pascal, or PL/I.

Continue entering that line and give a **CR** to end it, then enter the short line (STATES OF AMERICA), also followed by a **CR**. You are now at the start of the last line of your insertion, and since it is blank (as you want it to be) get out of insertion mode with an **ESC**.

Now add the second paragraph. You could do so by positioning your cursor at the end of the last line, giving an **a** command, and starting the appended text with a **CR**, which would immediately put you at the start of a new line. Since you want a blank line between the two paragraphs, you would then give a second **CR** (ending the first appended line), and start the next line with the three blanks. While this is not the best way of doing things, try it and get out of insertion mode with an **ESC** after entering a couple of words from the first text line. Now give a **u** command to undo the insertion. Note that the **u** command treats the whole insertion as one command (which it is) and so undoes it all.

The more usual way to append text is to position the cursor anywhere on the line after which you want to append, and give an

o command. This is just like the **O** command except that it adds text after the current line, whereas **O** adds it before the current line.

There is not much more to learn at this stage about entering text. What you need is practice. One last useful point could be demonstrated here. Enter the last two lines of the paragraph without a **CR** to separate them, i.e. as one line, before exiting the insertion mode. How can you change them into two lines? You have "... effect their ..." but you want "... effect**CR**their ...." The way to correct it should be clear when looked at this way: you want a **CR** in place of the blank. Put your cursor on the blank and give the command **rCR** which will do the trick.

Finally enter the last paragraph, correct any errors, and exit the editor. (See Sec. 3.2.) We will use this file repeatedly throughout the text so it is a good idea to make a copy of it in case you destroy the original. Give the command

    cp decl decl.arc

at the UNIX command prompt. The command **cp** is the copy command (it must be abbreviated, as the word copy will not work on most systems) and tells UNIX to copy the contents of the file decl (that you just made) into a new file called decl.arc. The letters after the period in the name are usually referred to as the extension of the file's name and usually indicate something about the kind of file it is; suggested are the letters arc to remind you that it is a backup or archival copy. If anything ever happens to your working copy of decl you can get a new copy by giving the command

    cp decl.arc decl

3.4 SUMMARY OF NEW COMMANDS

The following new commands were introduced in this chapter. Note that the first four are effective in insertion mode and the others in command mode.

Control–H	delete last input character (3.1)
Control–W	delete last input word (3.1)
erase	delete last character entered (3.1)
kill	delete input on this line (3.1)
–	move to first non–blank position on previous line (3.2)
A	append text at end of current line (3.2)
CR	move to first non–blank position on next line (3.2)
I	insert text at beginning of current line (3.2)
O	insert line above current line (3.3)
o	insert line below current line (3.3)

NOTES TO CHAPTER 3

1. You can redefine these keys with the UNIX **stty** command. However, do not do so; chaos will result when you ask a colleague, used to the local defaults, to do anything on your account.

2. Backspace or **Control–H** will erase in **vi** whether or not it is your system erase character. It is obviously much simpler to always use the same character.

3. In fact, get out of insertion mode to fix such an error immediately. Otherwise you may note errors and plan to fix them "as soon as I have finished this insertion," but forget to do so.

4. If you make any errors while entering the text, correct them using the methods described in Chap. 2.

5. How much depends on the speed of the communications link between your terminal and the computer.

4

Moving About
in vi

In the Prologue to this part I pointed out that editing consists of entering text, moving through it and modifying it. The last chapter emphasized entering text; this one will deal with moving through it. In addition to being important in its own right, this topic is essential to understanding the text modification commands.

4.1 OBJECTS

The editor recognizes a class of objects (rather large), which it deals with systematically. These include words, sentences, paragraphs, and other logical groupings. It also includes physical objects such as characters and lines. It also has a small set of operators, such as **d** (the deletion operator) and **c** (the change operator). These will act on any of the objects the editor knows. A command such as **dw** (introduced in Chap. 2) is interpreted as carrying out the delete operation on an object of type word. Once you know that, you can immediately conclude that **cw** will change a word, and that **yw** will do to a word whatever it is that **y** does (see Chap. 5 for what **y** does). This logical command structure makes **vi** much less confusing than it would otherwise be.

If you give a command consisting merely of an object, your cursor will move to that object. Hence in this chapter, in addition to learning how to move around, you will familiarize yourself with the fundamental objects.

4.2 FILE VERSUS SCREEN

There is an important point to note before you go any further. At any time there are two representations of the material you are editing: one in the computer and another, perhaps different one, on your screen. The reason for the occasional differences is efficiency: there are costs involved in modifying the screen's display. These costs depend on the smartness of your terminal and on the speed of the communications link between it and the computer. If you have a fast link to a smart terminal your screen may be updated almost immediately, while if you have a slower link or a less smart terminal (or both!), updates will be farther between.[1] An example of delayed updating is what often happens when you enter the command **cw** to change a word. The moment you enter that command the word is deleted from the computer's representation of your file, but it will probably remain on your screen till you either overwrite it completely or enter **ESC** to end your insertion. This saves both having to close up the space it occupied on the screen and making space for your insertion. Similarly, on many terminals, during insertion in the middle of pre-existing text, the material inserted appears to overwrite the original screen contents, avoiding constant updating of the display.

There are two other time saving features to note. If you delete a line you will probably find that while the text of that line disappears from the screen, the line is not filled up; instead, it will contain a solitary @ in the first position. This saves redrawing the screen. Also, unless you are using a fast terminal, you will find that the display does not normally fill the whole screen. This allows you to add lines at the top or bottom of the screen without the whole screen having to be redrawn. The number of lines initially displayed is called the window size. You may change it if you wish (Chap. 6).

Read this chapter for the first time sitting at a terminal, and try out everything that is suggested. Computing (as opposed to computer science) is learned behind a terminal, not in the library! (This is not really true, but it certainly does apply to learning how to use an editor).

As in the last chapter, give the command (at the UNIX level)

vi decl

to edit your Declaration of Independence file. The screen will fill up (perhaps only partly) and at the bottom you will get the message

"decl", 37 lines, 1468 characters

or something similar. The first line of text on the screen will be

IN CONGRESS, ...

with the cursor under the first letter.

4.3 MOVING LOCALLY

I find it useful to divide methods of moving into two groups: those used to move over short distances and the rather different ones used for longer distances.

4.31 Moving Over Characters and Words

You recall that hitting the space bar (referred to as **space**) will move you one character to the right, and that **dspace** will delete one character (the one the cursor is under). Hence it seems that **space** is the object "one character forward," and analogously **h** is "one character backward." How can you move many characters in either direction?

Suppose, to be specific, that you want to get your cursor on the "4" after "July" on the first line of your Declaration of Independence file. You can hit the space bar repeatedly, each time moving one position to the right. Another way is to estimate that you need to move over about 20 positions. The command **20space** will move you 20 positions to the right, to the blank before the year. This is another important feature of **vi**: a number preceding an object is taken to be a count of how many items of that kind are to be processed. Hence **20space** means 20 characters. There are far better ways of moving over multiple spaces than counting, or guessing, the number of spaces, but introduced here is an important concept. Can you guess what **d20space** means? Try it out and see if you guessed right (use **u** to undo its effect).

Now return to the start of that line[2] and enter **w** (which, you may recall, was used to refer to words when using the delete and change commands). The cursor is now positioned under the "C" of "CONGRESS." Try a second **w**. You expected to get to July, did you not? That would have meant treating the comma as part of the word "CONGRESS." Is it really part of the word? It depends. If you want to change a word you will usually want the punctuation mark that follows it to remain in place, while if you want to move through a line of text you may well want to skip over both the word and the following punctuation mark.

While still on the comma following "CONGRESS" enter **4w**. That is clearly a command to move forward four words. Where will it take you to? The first word will take you to "July," the second to "4," the third to the comma following it, and the final one to the start of "1776." Now give the command **3w**. Unlike the **space** and **h** commands, this one does take you past the end of the line, to the start of "UNANIMOUS." That only seems to be two words away; what happened? Get back to the start of line 1 with two successive − commands. Give single **w** commands, watching where each one takes you, till you get to the start of 1776. Note that the next **w** takes you to the start of the blank second line, showing that the editor considers a blank line to be a word!

Since you can move forward in steps of words, you should be able to move backward the same way. Indeed, the **b** (for back) command will back you up one or more words, just like the **w** command will move you forward. To round things out, there is an **e** command that will move you to the end of the current word. Try all of them out, with and without repetition counts.

The definition of a word used by these three commands is a collection of letters and numbers, or a sequence of special characters (punctuation marks and the various symbols used in programming language). So something like "abc/def//ghi" consists of no fewer than five words: "abc," "/," "def," "//," and finally "ghi." Return to the first line, enter this expression above it (with an **O** command), and try it out.

There is a second definition of a word, a sequence of non–blank characters separated by one or more blank characters (a blank character is a space, a tab, or the end of the line).[3] Hence the above collection of symbols would be one word by that definition. To refer to such "big words" use the same commands, only use capitals, so **W** will move you forward, **B** will move you back, and **E** will move you to the end of a big word. Obviously here again you can specify how many big words you want to move over in either direction. Try these six commands (entering examples of your own to try them out on) till you are sure you understand exactly how they work. When you are through, delete the added lines. You want to keep your file clean.

If your terminal supports keyboard repeat (see Sec. 1.2) you should try it out with the commands described above. You may find it a very useful feature if your terminal repeats at a reasonably slow rate; at fast rates of repetition it is difficult to control accurately.

4.3.2 Moving to Specified Positions

One often wants to move to the beginning or end of a line. Get to the start of the original first line and give the command **$**. It will take you to the end of that line. Now give a **0** (the number zero) command. It will take you back to the start of that line. Give a second **$** and follow it this time with a **^** command. This will also take you to the start of the line. Are they identical commands? Not really. Try the same exercise on the first line of the text of the declaration. In this case **0** will take you to the start of the line, while **^** will only take you back to the start of the first word (WHEN).

The command **0** always takes you to the first column of the screen (column zero, since computer people usually count up from zero). On the other hand, ∧ takes you back to the first non–blank position on the line. Why ∧? In most cases, you are more likely to want to do something to the first word than to the blanks that may precede it, and that is where the command gets you. This is especially applicable to programs, where many lines will start with one or more blanks and you are more likely to want to get on the first "real" (i.e., non–blank) character than on the preceding blanks (spaces or tabs).

When the cursor is on a tab it sits on the last of the several spaces that represent the tab. Thus if your line starts with a tab, the command **0** will put the cursor on the eighth column of the screen (which is blank), and **x** will delete the tab. On the other hand, ∧ will put the cursor on the non–blank character in column nine; backspacing with **h** will move it back one column, and further attempts to backspace will produce beeps, since you are already on the first character of that line.

A related command that will move the cursor to any physically specified location on a line is the | command. Thus **50|** will move you to column 50 of the screen. Columns are counted starting from one (not zero), hence **1|** has the same effect as **0**. Furthermore, if you give the command with an argument larger than the length of the line, the cursor will go to the end of the line without complaining.

This command is useful if you have long lines that you want to split. Splitting lines is easily accomplished by putting the cursor on an appropriate blank space and giving the command **rCR**, which replaces the space by a **CR**. Thus if you do not want any lines much longer than 72 characters in your file, and as a result of insertions you have a line that is longer, you can use **70|** to get you to column 70, where you can move to the most convenient space and replace it by a **CR**.

4.3.3 Local Searches

The last way of specifically moving within a line is with the local search commands. Typing **f** (for find) followed by a single character will move the cursor to the next occurrence of that character on the line you are on. If that character does not appear on the current line you will get a beep and the cursor will remain where it was. This command is especially useful if there is a punctuation mark or uncommon character near the place you are trying to get to. Move to the start of the line that reads

that among these are Life, Liberty and the pursuit

and give the command

fL

The cursor should move to the "L" of "Life." The editor will remember the last character you used with a local search command, and at any time after that, giving a single **;** will move you forward to the next occurrence of that pattern (on the line you are on). If you overshoot, **,** will get you back. Try them both out: giving a **;** command will get you to the "L" of "Liberty," and from there a **,** will get you back to "Life." A second **,** will give you a beep and leave the cursor where it is, as there is no "L" on that line before the cursor. Now move up to the line that reads

THE UNANIMOUS DECLARATION of the thirteen united

and give a **;** command. The cursor will move to the "L" of "DECLARATION," showing that the character searched for is remembered even if you move off the line you were on when you first gave the command. To move backward to the previous occurrence of a character, enter **F**; to go further back again use **;**. Both **f** and **F** (as well as **;** and **,**) can be preceded by a count. Move back to the start of the line with "Life" and give the command

2fL

It will move you to the "L" of "Liberty."

Both **f** and **F** move you to the character searched for, which is usually what you want. If you are using local searches in conjunction with operations such as deletion (Chap. 5) you may wish to delete up to (but not including) the character. The commands **t** (short for *to*) and **T** will move you (forward and backward respectively) up to, but not on, the character given. Once again get to the start of the "Life" line, and give the command

tL

It will put the cursor under the space before "Life." They are of little use in moving, but are often used in making deletions and changes.

Here you have an example of a principle that you will often see in **vi**. There are two similar commands, **f** and **F**, one of which works forward, i.e., going down the file, while the other goes backward, i.e., up the file. They are invoked by the same letter, in upper case to go up and in lower case to go down.[4] This simplifies remembering the many commands that **vi** has. Note that this principle does not apply universally; the opposite of **w** is **b**, not **W**!

4.3.4 Summary of Local Motion Commands

Now to summarize the commands that can move you within a line. **Space** and **h** will move you forward or backward in units of characters; **0**, **^**, and **$** will move you to the beginning or end of the line; **|** will move you to a specified position within it. These commands are based on what you might think of as hard physical representations of text. Then there are the word commands, which move you over words, defined in two ways. Words represent a higher level of structure in your text. Finally, **f**, **F**, **t**, and **T** will move you to (or before) a specific symbol.

4.4 MOVING OVER LONGER DISTANCES

The commands that will take you from one line to another show the same hierarchy that exists for movements within a line. Some deal with physical objects: lines, screenfuls, and the like. Others deal with higher structures: sentences, paragraphs, and sections. Finally, there are commands that search for specific text patterns, longer than the single character that **f** and related commands search for.

4.4.1 Using Physical Units

You are already familiar with two commands that work at the lowest physical level: **j** will move you down while **k** will move you up, by one line if given alone, or by as many lines as you want if you precede the command by the number of lines you want to move. Both **j** and **k** will try to stay in the column they started out in. If, however, they get to a line that does not extend to the position they started out in, they will take the cursor to the end of that line. On reaching a suitably long line they will once again put the cursor in the column it started out in. Move to the line that reads

all men are created equal, that they are endowed

and get to the comma with a **f,** command. Give a **k** command and the cursor will move up to the "o" of "to" in the previous line. A second **k** will move you to the start of the previous (blank) line; a further **k** will move you to the period at the end of the previous line, while a final **k** will at last get you back on the column you started out in, under the "a" of "causes".

Often you will want the cursor to move up or down along the left hand margin of the screen. One obvious way to do so is to get it there with a **0** or **^** command, and then move it up or down with the **j** and **k** commands. Alternately, a **+** or **CR** will move the cursor down to the first non-blank position of the next line; **CR** is easier than **+** and should be used. To go up the same way, use **−**. There are no corresponding commands to go up or down the first column of the screen.

There are three commands that can move you to specified lines on the current screen display. **H** will move the cursor to the "home" position, at the start of the top line on the current screen. Entering **5H** will move you to the fifth line on the current screen. The opposite command is **L**, which will take you to the last line of the screen; **5L** will take you to the fifth line from the bottom. Finally **M** will take you to the middle of the screen; it obviously does not take a count.

So far you have been looking at more or less local commands, the kind you would use to get to a word or letter that needs to be

modified. There will be times when you will want to scan the text
you have entered, either to check for general correctness or to
look for an error whose location you are not sure of. In either case,
Control–D will scroll down the file, and **Control–U** will scroll up
the file. Try them both. The number of lines they scroll up or
down depends on the size of your screen window, which in turn
depends on the speed of your terminal. You can change the
number of lines scrolled (without changing the window size) by
preceding the scroll command by a number; thus **10Control–D**
will scroll down 10 lines. Furthermore, the number of lines
scrolled (in either direction) will now be reset to 10. **Control–F***
will move about one page forward, erasing the current page and
drawing the next one, keeping the bottom two lines of the
previous page; it moves faster than **Control–D** but gives a more
discontinuous feel. **Control–B*** will move a corresponding page
backward. Giving a count to **Control–F** or **Control–B** will tell the
computer how many pages to move.

Less useful commands are **Control–E***, which will expose
one more line at the bottom of the page, and **Control–Y*** which
will do the same at the top. Finally, **Control–P** will move the cursor
to the corresponding position on the previous line (like **k**), and
Control–N or **Control–J** will move it to the next line (like **j**). To
complete this section, add that **Control–H** is a synonym for plain
h. None of these synonyms seems to have anything to recommend
it; they are mentioned for the sake of completeness.

There are a few ways of moving to specific lines. While not
shown on the screen, part of the internal representation of each
line is its number, in a sequence that starts with 1 for the first line
and increases by one. The command n**G** will take you to line n of
your file (**G** alone will take you to the last line). You can find the
number of the line you are on with the command **Control–G**. Try
it. In addition to printing the line number, it will print the name of
the file, the number of lines in it, and the percent of the way
through it that you are. Having noted the number of the line you
are on, do a **G** command to get to the end of the file. Now use a

---

*This command is not present in all versions of the editor. Throughout this book, all
commands (whether editor or UNIX) that may be absent, or function differently, on
certain systems will be marked with an asterisk. These differences will be discussed in App.
E.

second **G** command, with the number of the line you were on, to get back there.

Line numbers are not a very useful tool, as the insertion or deletion of a single line will affect the numbers of all lines following the change. A much more useful way to move to a specific place in your text is to mark it. Before doing the following, find the ` (reverse single quote) key on your terminal.

Move to the third word of the last line of the file (with a **G** command followed by **3w**), and enter **1G** to get to the top of the file. Now enter ` ` (two back quotes), and your cursor will return to its previous position. This is a very useful tool, especially when an erroneous command takes you very far from where you were (and want to be). Note that if you move down five lines with a **5j** command, you cannot get back with the ` `, since your new location is the one that command refers to. Its use is to return after commands like **G** and the search commands that we will discuss later.

As you noted, the ` ` command returns your cursor to its previous position. A related command, " (two single quotes), will return your cursor to the start of the line it was on. Go again to the top of the file, and this time use a " command to return. You will find that your cursor is now on the first character of the last line.

You can mark the current position of your cursor in a way that will allow you to refer to it at any later time. This is done with the **m** (for mark) command, followed by a letter. Thus **m***x* will associate the mark *x* with the position of the cursor at the time you gave the command. Return to the third word on the last line, and give the command **ma**. Nothing visible will happen, but the mark **a** will have been associated with your current position. Now move up a few lines with the − command; you will no longer be able to return to your position on the last line with a ` ` command. Now go to the top of the file and enter `**a** (note again, back quote!). You should be back where you started. The mark will not be affected by any lines you may add or remove from the file, and is a far better mechanism for referring to specific lines than are line numbers. You can refer to the line on which the mark is (rather than to its exact position) by using an ordinary single quote; thus '**a** will get you to the first position on the line containing the mark. You will find the distinction important when doing deletions and changes.

4.4.2 Using Logical Objects

Having learned the ways of moving in physical units, you will now learn to move in larger logical units: sentences, paragraphs, or sections. A sentence is defined as ending at a **.**, **!**, or **?** which is followed by either the end of a line or by two spaces. Note that two spaces are needed to mark the end of a sentence; this makes it easier to deal with abbreviations, when you generally have only one space before the next character. Any number of closing **)**, **}**, **"** characters may appear after the **.**, **!**, or **?** and before the spaces or end of line. A paragraph is defined as beginning after a blank line, or on a paragraph definition used by the document formatting system. The end of a paragraph is also a sentence end. Sections are defined as starting at a section macro definition used by the document formatter. Section boundaries are also sentence and paragraph boundaries. As a convenience to C programmers a line starting with a **{** is considered a section start, some commands will treat a line starting with **}** as a section end (rather than searching for the next line starting with **{** and treating it as a section start).

A **)** will get you to the beginning of the next sentence. Similarly, **}** will get you to the beginning of the next paragraph, and **]]**[5] to the beginning of the next section. To go back to the beginning of the object you are on, use the opposite symbol, thus **(** will get you to the start of the current sentence (or previous sentence if you are already on the start of the current one). There is no command to get you to the end of the current object.

4.4.3 Searching

The final way of moving around is by searching for a specific pattern (a word or an expression in a program). This is probably the main way you will use for moving over longer distances. The command **/**_pat_**CR** will search forwards in the file until it finds the first occurrence of the pattern _pat_.

Let's attempt to find the word "Liberty" in your Declaration of Independence file. First, move to the top of the file using the command **1G**. Then enter a slash (**/**). You will note that the slash appears on the bottom line of the screen. Now enter the word

"Liberty." It will appear, following the slash, on the last line. Finally, terminate the command by entering **CR** or **ESC**.[6] Depending on the window size, the text will either scroll until the line containing that pattern is reached, or the screen will be redrawn around it. In either case, the cursor will be under the first letter.

There is no need to use the complete word; the search command will search for the first occurrence of a pattern in the file. That pattern can be a complete word, as in this example. It can also be part of a word. To demonstrate, return to the top of the file and give the command

/LibCR

Once again the cursor will be under the "L" of "Liberty." This is because that is the first occurrence of the pattern "Lib" in the file. Now return to the top of the file and try to abbreviate the pattern further, giving the command

/Li

This time the cursor will be under the "L" of "Life," as this is the first occurrence of the pattern you are now searching for.

Entering **?** before the string will search backward from where you are, and is otherwise similar to **/**. The editor remembers the last search pattern you gave it, and to go to the next occurrence of the pattern you just found you need only enter **n** (for next).[7] Furthermore, not only does the editor remember what the last string you searched for was, but it also remembers in which direction you searched for it. Hence the command **n** will search for that string in the same direction as you last searched for it. The command **N** will search for the string in the opposite direction to that of the initial search.

Note that the search may not get you to where you wanted to go. If you want to go to the word "there" and only entered **/the/** you may well end up on a "the" that is either that word, or the start of "they," or something similar that occurred before the word you wanted to get to. If the string you are searching for is not present in your document, you will get the message "pattern not found" on the bottom line, and the cursor will not move. Note that under normal circumstances the search "wraps around" the end of the document if it does not find the pattern before. That is, if you are searching in the forward direction and the pattern does not occur before the end of the file, the search will continue from the start of the file.

The **vi** editor has a very sophisticated set of searching capabilities that you will explore in greater detail in Chaps. 8 and 10. Note here that it is possible to require that the pattern being searched for be at the beginning of a line by preceding it with the up-arrow ^. Similarly, you can search for a pattern at the end of a line by following it by **$.**

Searches, like marks, refer to a specific position within a line. They may, however, be used to refer to lines. In this case you have to follow the pattern by a second delimiter (**/** or **?**) and a count; thus **/pat/ + 3** will move you to the start of the third line after that on which *pat* was found, while **/pat/ + 0** will move you to the start of the line containing it. This is more often used in connection with modifications than for moving around.

It is possible (though rarely very useful) to carry out compound searches. For example, **/elementary/;/Watson/** will search for the first occurrence of Watson after the first occurrence of elementary. It is good to know that this capability exists, but in most cases one will do two searches.

4.5 SUMMARY OF NEW COMMANDS

The following are the new commands studied in this chapter. Those marked with an asterisk are not found in all versions of the editor.

Control-B*   move backward one page (4.4.1)
Control-D   scroll down (4.4.1)
Control-E*   expose one more line at bottom of screen (4.4.1)
Control-F*   move forward one page (4.4.1)
Control-G   print statistics on current file and position (4.4.1)
Control-H   move back one space (**h** better) (4.4.1)
Control-J   same as **j**, which is better (4.4.1)
Control-N   same as **j**, which is better (4.4.1)
Control-P   same as **k**, which is better (4.4.1)

Control-U	scroll up (4.4.1)
Control-Y*	expose one more line at top of screen (4.4.1)
B	move to start of current big word (4.3.1)
E	move to end of current big word (4.3.1)
Fx	move backward to x on current line (4.3.3)
n**G**	move to start of line n (4.4.1)
H	move to start of top line on current screen (4.4.1)
L	move to start of last line on current screen (4.4.1)
M	move to start of middle line on current screen (4.4.1)
N	search for pattern in opposite direction (4.4.3)
Tx	move backward to after x on current line (4.3.3)
W	move to start of next big word (4.3.1)
b	move to start of current word (4.3.1)
e	move to end of current word (4.3.1)
fx	move forward to x on current line (4.3.3)
mx	associate a mark (x) with current position (4.4.1)
n	search for pattern in same direction (4.4.3)
tx	move forward to before x on current line (4.3.3)
w	move to start of next word (4.3.1)
CR	move to first non-blank character on next line (4.4.1)
$	move to end of current line (4.3.2)
"	return to start of line you were previously on (4.4.1)
'x	move to start of line containing mark x (4.4.1)
(	move to start of current sentence (4.4.2)
)	move to start of next sentence (4.4.2)
+	move to first non-blank on character next line (**CR** better) (4.4.1)
,	move to previous occurrence of symbol searched for with **f** or **F** on current line (4.3.3)
-	move to first non-blank character on previous line (4.4.1)
/patCR	move forward to first occurrence of pattern *pat* (4.4.3)

0	move to start of current line (4.3.2)
;	move to next occurrence of symbol searched for with **f** or **F** on current line (4.3.3)
?patCR	move backward to first occurrence of pattern *pat* (4.4.3)
[[	move to start of current section (4.4.2)
]]	move to start of next section (4.4.2)
∧	move to first non-blank character on current line (4.3.2)
`x	go to position marked *x* (4.4.1)
``	return to previous position (4.4.1)
{	move to start of current paragraph (4.4.2)
n|	move to column *n* on current line (4.3.2)
}	move to start of next paragraph (4.4.2)

NOTES TO CHAPTER 4

1. This is one of the editor functions that you can set according to your preference. Before changing the setting selected at your installation (Chap. 6), you should realize that those who selected it had a good reason for doing so.

2. How? If **20space** took you 20 spaces forward, **20h** should clearly take you 20 spaces backward.

3. Space, tabs, and the end of the line (referred to in the UNIX literature as **newline**), when used as separators, are often grouped together as **white space.**

4. You saw an example of this principle in the previous chapter, where it was noted that **o** will add lines below the current line, while **O** will add them above the current line.

5. Note that this requires **two** square brackets. The idea is that since this instruction may take you far afield, especially if your sections are large, it should be difficult to enter it accidentally. Compare to the use of **ZZ** used to get out of the editor.

6. A command which appears on the bottom line of the screen and that needs a **CR** or **ESC** to terminate it is an **ex** command even when, as in this case, it is not preceded by a colon. Searching will be discussed in greater detail (in the context of **vi**) in Sec. 8.1, while it will be discussed in the **ex** context in Chap. 10.

7. Note that another way of searching for the same pattern is just to enter **/CR**. This is longer than **n** and would not normally be used. It is often used accidentally: you enter **/** to start searching for a pattern, pause to think, decide not to enter that pattern, and hit **ESC**, which acts like **CR** in this case. To cancel the start of a search, either backspace over the entire bottom line or kill the search with **INT**.

5

Deleting, Changing, and Moving Text

This chapter is a continuation of Chap. 4, and like it should be studied sitting at a terminal editing the **decl** file. Every command described should be tried out, and those which seem tricky should be played around with till they are totally clear to you. The number of specific examples given will decrease, as you should be able to develop your own by now. In Chap. 4 you became familiar with the kinds of objects used by the editor. You will find that learning how to use them for deleting, changing, and moving text is easy.

5.1 DELETING AND CHANGING

Deleting and changing are very similar operations, as changing is accomplished by deletion followed by insertion. These commands operate on the text objects studied in Chap. 4, ranging from characters to entire sections.

The simplest of these commands is **x**, which will delete the character under the cursor and bring the next character over the cursor. The simplest of the change commands corresponding to **x** is **r**, for replace. It will replace the character under the cursor by the next character entered, and unlike most other change commands will not put you in the insertion mode. Preceding it by a count will replace that number of characters by the single character that you enter. Thus **5rb** will replace 5 characters by b, which is probably not what you intended! If you want to replace several characters by overtyping, use the **R** command. It will put you into insertion mode and will replace the characters that you type over till you hit **ESC**. It is useful when you want to replace a few characters by an equal number of characters; for instance, to change include into exclude.

The most commonly used deletion and change commands are **d** and **c**, which will delete or change the objects named in the command. You saw in Chap. 2 how to use the commands to delete or change characters, words, and lines; they also act on the more complex objects described in Chap. 4, and have a variety of shorter synonyms for common commands.

The format is uniform, consisting of the command, followed by the object on which it is to act, and optionally preceded by a count. As an example, **5dw**[1] will delete five words, starting with the word the cursor is on. The object acted on can be any of the following.

5.1.1 Characters

To delete or change one or more characters on the current line, enter the appropriate command followed by a space, preceded by an optional count. Thus **3d** followed by a space will delete three characters starting from the one under the cursor, while **4c** followed by a space will delete the next four characters and put you into insertion mode (where you can enter as many characters as you want; you are not limited by the number of characters removed). Note that they will not delete characters beyond the end of the current line; if there are only five characters after the cursor on the current line no more than five will be deleted, whatever count you give to **d** or **c**. Both of these commands have single key synonyms: it was noted above that **x** is a synonym for delete character, and **s** (substitute) is a synonym for change character.

Actually, **x** is not exactly a synonym for **dspace**, since it behaves differently if it is near the end of a line and given a repetition count greater than the number of remaining characters on the line. If the cursor is on the last character of a line, it will delete it and move back to the previous character. If preceded by a count, it will delete that number of characters, starting from the one under the cursor. What happens if you are on the third character from the end of a line and you give the instruction **5x**? Move to the first line of the **decl** file

IN CONGRESS, July 4, 1776

and move to the first "7." Give five successive **x** commands; the first three will delete the "776," with the cursor now under the 1. The fourth **x** will remove the "1," leaving the cursor under the blank, while the fifth **x** will remove the blank. Undo all these changes with the **U** command (see Sec. 5.2). The line will be restored to its initial state, with the cursor at its start. Return to the first "7," and give the command **5x**; it will delete the "1776" and the preceding blank, leaving the cursor under the comma. Undo it with a simple **u** command. Now return again to the first "7," give the command **5dspace**, and note that unlike **5x** this only deletes the three remaining characters on the line. Do not forget to undo that last change!

A less commonly used command is **X**, which will delete the single character before[2] the cursor. Another very useful command is ~*, which will change the case of the character under the cursor, if it is alphabetic. It then positions the cursor over the next character. It does not take a preceding count, but as it moves the cursor it is easy to use it to change the case of short pieces of text. It has no effect on nonalphabetic characters.

---

*This command is not present in all versions of the editor. Throughout this book, all commands (whether editor or UNIX) that may be absent, or function differently, on certain systems will be marked with an asterisk. These differences will be discussed in App. E.

5.1.2 Words

You have met both **dw** and **cw** in Chap. 2, where it was noted that the former deletes a word and the space that follows it (i.e., deletes until the start of the next word), while the latter only deletes the word you are on, putting you into insertion mode. Hence, to be logically consistent, the latter command should really be called **ce** (change to the end of the word we are on), a command that does produce exactly the same result. Why then does **cw** work the way it does? Because the designers of **vi** decided to choose what most users think a **cw** command would do rather than what a rigorous application of the definition would give.

Either **dw** or **cw** can be preceded by a count. The definition of a word is the same as that used for moving (Chap. 4), and you similarly can act on "ordinary" or "big" words, using **W** in the latter case. Again, **db** will delete backwards; i.e., it will delete to the start of the word you are in, or, if you are on the start of a word, it will delete to the start of the previous word. In either case, the character the cursor is on will be left. This is an example of the general rule just noted. Once again you can use **B** instead of **b** to delete a "big" word backwards. While these commands are among the most frequently used, they do not have any synonyms.

Unlike character oriented deletes and changes, the word oriented ones act across lines. Thus if you are two words from the end of a line and issue the command **4dw**, the last two words of that line and the first two of the next one are deleted. A result of this is that the two lines are joined, giving a long line that will probably need to be split. The cursor will be positioned at the end of what remains of the first line (a blank), where you can give a **rCR** to split the line.

These commands are not quite as smart as you might wish, though they do what you want most of the time. Thus if you are in the middle of a word **dw** will not delete it; it merely deletes from the cursor to the start of the next word.[3] You will therefore be left with the remains of the word you were on, followed immediately by the next word. This is not a suitable way of chopping off parts of words. That can be accomplished using the **de** command to delete to the end of the current word. Again, if the word is followed by a punctuation mark, you will be left with the space following the previous word followed by the punctuation mark. It is not too difficult to clean up any mess that remains if you are alert and look at the screen.

Spend some time trying out delete and change commands with "ordinary" and "big" words at the beginning, middle, and end of lines, until you are sure that you know what they do. If you mess up the file beyond your ability to correct it, leave it with a **:q!** (Sec. 2.5) command.

5.1.3 Lines

There are several commands that are line-oriented. The simplest are **dd** and **cc**, which will delete or change the entire line they are on. Again, preceding either by a count will make it act on that number of lines. The command **S** is a synonym for **cc** and may be thought of as a substitute acting on lines rather than on characters, as **s** does.

Alternately, you may wish to delete or change the rest of the line you are on; the obvious way to do so is with **d$** or **c$** (remembering that **$** refers to the end of the current line). Synonyms exist for both of these commands; they are **D** and **C** (note the analogy with **A**). You might expect that giving a **D** command with the cursor at the beginning of a line would delete the line. In fact, it deletes text on the line but not the end of line character that ends it, and thus leaves a blank line.

Correspondingly, **d0** or **s0** will delete or change from the start of the line to (but not including) the current position of the cursor; they do not have any synonyms. The very similar **d^** and **c^** commands do the same, without affecting any leading blanks.

There are still further ways of deleting (or changing) ranges of lines, which correspond to the various ways of moving to given lines. You learned in Chap. 4 that **L** will move you to the last line on the current screen and **dL** will delete text to the last line on the current screen, while **d4L** will delete text until the fourth line from the bottom of the screen. The same, of course, applies to **H**, which represents the top of the screen. You can also use line numbers; thus **d23G** will delete text (in the appropriate direction) from the current line to line 23.

5.1.4 Sentences, Paragraphs, and Sections

In Chap. 4 sentences, paragraphs, and sections were defined. Both **d** and **c** can act on these objects, going either forward or backward. Thus **d)** will delete to the start of the next sentence, while **d{** will delete from the start of the current paragraph up to, but not including, the character the cursor is on. Note once again that the definition of the end of a sentence is a period followed by either a new line or by two blanks. If you leave only one blank after each sentence, **vi** will not recognize them as sentences. Note also that the definition of a paragraph or section header depends on the word processing macros that you are using; in Chap. 6 you will see how you can specify the set you are using.

5.1.5 Other Objects

Any kind of object studied in the previous chapter can be either deleted or changed. A few more examples will be mentioned here, but the basic rule is that if entering an expression will move you to somewhere in the file, entering **d** followed by that expression will delete material from where you are to where the expression would have taken you.

One group of often used objects consists of patterns searched for with **/**: thus **d/*pat*CR** will delete text from the position of the cursor to the start of *pat*. If you want to delete whole lines from the current line to that containing *pat,* you must enter **d/*pat*/ + 0CR,** which operates on lines. Needless to say, **?** operates identically in the opposite direction.

Deletions and changes can be specified using the intra–line search commands, **f** and **F.** Thus **df,** will delete from (including) the current position of the cursor up to (and including) the next comma, if there is one on the current line. If there is no comma after the cursor on that line, you will get a beep and the cursor will stay where it was. Similarly, **dF.** will delete everything from the preceding period to the current cursor position, including the period, but excluding the character the cursor was on (do you remember the general rule?). You may well wish to leave the period in and delete backwards up to but not including it; you have a pair of modifiers, **t** and **T**, which will cause deletion up to, but not including, the character following them. As you might expect, **t** acts forward while **T** acts backwards. In all cases the deletion only occurs if the character is found on that line, searching in the appropriate direction. If it is not found the terminal will beep at you and the cursor will remain in its original position.

Another common kind of deletion or change involves marks. You saw in Chap. 4 how you could mark a given position and be able to return to it later. To do so you moved the cursor to it and entered **m**x if you wanted to mark it as x (any lower case letter will do). You can return to that position from anywhere in your file by entering **'**x. Similarly, you can delete up to (or from) that position to the cursor using **d**`x (reverse single quote). You also have a line-oriented delete, **d'**x (single quote), which will delete lines from the line on which the cursor is to the line on which the mark is.

A final type of deletion or change involves positions on the screen. If you have tabular material and want to delete the first three columns, which extend to column 17, the command **d17|** will do it. That is not very useful if done to a single line, since you would have to figure out the column from which you want to delete. If, however, you will want to make this change on all the lines of a table, that command given once, together with the repeat command described in the next section, may well be the fastest way to do it.

5.1.6 Two Miscellaneous Commands

As a result of changes, you may have lines that are either much longer or much shorter than you want. The classical way to shorten a line is to replace a suitable space with a **CR**, and you saw in Chap. 4 that a | could get you to a column close to where you wanted the line to end. The opposite command, to join two lines, is **J**. This is a pretty smart command, as it appends a space at the end of the first line. If, however, that line ends with a period (end of sentence), it will put two spaces between the end of the first line and the start of the second to keep the end of sentence clear.

The second item is not really a command but a way of repeating the last command that changed the file. This is done by entering a period in the command mode. If you have just deleted a word and want to delete a second one, you can enter **.** rather than **dw,** saving yourself a keystroke. This is especially useful for repetitive changes or insertions. If, for instance, you have a C or Pascal program with many missing terminal semicolons, simply get to the first line with a missing semicolon and enter **A;ESC**. Then go to the next line and enter **.**, it will append a semicolon to the end of the line and return to command mode.

5.1.7 WARNING: The Curse of the Stray d

Imagine the following: You are in the middle of a long document, and have started to delete something. You have just entered the first **d** and stopped to think. Finally you decide not to delete it, but to move instead to the end of the document and add some more text. You therefore enter a **G** and to your dismay read "300 lines deleted" or something similar. What happened? The computer received the command **dG**, and the fact that the two parts of it were separated by a time interval is not relevant. Hence it deleted text to the end of the file. Of course, the same thing could have happened with a **c** command. If you are alert you can detect this and recover with a **u**. However, if you are engrossed in thought you may lose a large portion of your file.

The object of this warning is to make you aware of the danger of stray **d**s. Hit **ESC** when you start a command and decide not to give it. In fact, whenever you have any doubt about what mode you are in, hit **ESC**. It will never do any harm and can keep you out of trouble!

5.2 MOVING AND UNDELETING TEXT: THE BUFFERS

You have noted the very important **u** command, which will undo the last command given. Suppose you have been making several changes to a single line and finally conclude that its original form was better than any of your "improvements." You cannot recover it by a simple **u**, which will merely undo the last change. However, **U** will undo all changes made on the current line since you got to it. Note that you cannot use it if you have moved from the line after last modifying it. It is less used than **u**, but is very useful when needed.

Did you ever wonder how text that has been deleted can be

restored using the **u** command? Obviously, it must have been stored somewhere after its "deletion." There are nine auxiliary buffers, numbered one to nine, in which deleted text is stored. The most recently deleted text is always stored in buffer number one, the previously deleted text in buffer number two, and so on. The contents of any of these buffers can be put back into the main buffer by using the put command. That command comes in two flavors: **p** will put material after the cursor, while **P** will put material before it. This is not quite accurate, since material that has been deleted as lines will be put either before or after the line on which the cursor is, while other material will be inserted into the line on which the cursor is. If you do not precede the **p** command with a buffer number, the contents of buffer number one are put.

This gives you a very simple way of correcting one of the commonest forms of typing errors, transpositions. Suppose that you have typed "sipmle" instead of "simple." How do you correct it? The most obvious way would be to put the cursor on the "p" and give an **RmpESC** command. A slightly simpler way is to give the sequence **xp** of commands. The **x** will remove the "p" and store it in the buffer, moving the cursor over to the next letter, the "m." Then the **p** command will put the deleted "p" in its place, after the "m." The saving in effort is small—two keystrokes instead of four—but it is a very good illustration of how to combine commands.[4]

To put the contents of any other buffer, precede the command by a double quote[5] and the buffer number; thus **"3p** will put the contents of the third buffer after the cursor or current line.

What do you do if you want to restore text but do not know which buffer it is in? The obvious way is to start by **"1p**. If it returns the text you wanted, well and good. Otherwise try **u"2p**, first undoing the restoration, then trying out the contents of the second buffer, and so on till you find your text. There is a simpler way of doing it, involving the **.** command. Normally it just repeats the previous change command. However, if that command involves a numbered buffer, it will increment the buffer number before each execution. So the sequence **"1pu.u.u.** will put the text in the fourth buffer before (or above) your cursor.

While **p** is useful for restoring text that has been accidentally deleted, its main use is to move text from one location to another by intentionally deleting it and then putting it in its new location. To put the second paragraph of **decl** after the last paragraph, get to the blank line of the second paragraph. A good way of getting there from the top of the file is with the } command, as a blank line delimits a paragraph. Once there give a **d}** command to delete to the end of the paragraph. You will have deleted the blank line and the second paragraph. Now get to the end of the file with a **G** command followed by a **p** command, to put the deleted text after what was originally the last paragraph.

This example was chosen to show the delete and put combination to its best advantage, as lines are the easiest objects to move about. Should you wish to move a sentence, rather than a sequence of lines, you may have some cosmetic problems after you put it at its new destination, such as no space between the end of the moved sentence and the start of the following one. These are easily fixed, as long as you inspect the result of your work.

There are 26 named buffers (named **a-z**) that you can directly address, deleting text into them or putting it from them. To do so, precede the delete or put command by **"x**, where *x* is the name of the buffer that you want to use. Thus to restore **decl** to its initial state you could specifically use buffer **a**, deleting the original third paragraph into it with a **"ad}** command, and putting it in its place with a **"ap** command. Note the double quote before the **a**; if omitted the editor would believe that you were starting an append command! It is always wise to use a named buffer unless you plan to put the text back immediately. If you plan to move text from one file to another (see Chap. 7) you *must* use a named buffer, as the numbered buffers are lost when changing files.

When you delete something into a named buffer using a lower case letter, the previous contents of that buffer are erased. In most cases that is exactly what you want. Using an upper case letter will append the deleted material to the end of the named buffer. This is very useful when you want to collect all lines showing a given pattern together. The first line would be deleted into buffer *x* using **d***x* to clear the buffer. Subsequent lines would be added using **d***X*, appending them to the end of the buffer. After you have collected all the lines you want, you can put them all out together with a **p***x* or **p***X* command, as case has no significance when putting.

The delete command is inappropriate when you want to duplicate text without losing the original. There is a command, **y** (for yank), which will copy the object it acts on into a buffer without removing it. Objects are defined exactly as for the delete command, except that to yank a line you can either use **yy** or the more convenient synonym **Y**.

Yank is very useful in writing programs when you want to have almost identical code in two different places. You enter it once, yank it, and put it in the second location and modify it. It is also useful in any situation in which you want more than one version of nearly identical material.

5.3 SUMMARY OF NEW COMMANDS

The following are the new commands studied in this chapter. Those marked with an asterisk are not found in all versions of the editor.

C	change to end of line (5.1.3)
D	delete to end of line (5.1.3)
J	join next line to current one smartly (5.1.6)
P	put contents of a buffer into text before cursor (5.2)
R	replace characters by overtyping (5.1)
S	change line (5.1.3)
U	undo all current changes on current line (5.2)
X	delete character before cursor (5.1.1)
Y	copy current line into buffer (5.2)
P	put contents of a buffer into text after cursor (5.2)
s	change character (5.1.1)
y	copy object into buffer (5.2)
.	repeat last command which changed buffer (5.1.6)
~*	change case of character if alphabetic (5.1.1)

NOTES TO CHAPTER 5

1. **d5w** will have the same effect.

2. Note that repeated use of **X** will delete backwards, thus **10X** will remove the ten characters before the current position of the cursor, leaving the character under the cursor unchanged. On the other hand, **10x** will remove the character under the cursor and the nine succeeding ones. You will find that this is an example of a general rule: operators which delete forward remove the character under the cursor; those that delete backward leave it.

NOTE: Not available in all versions of the editor.

3. If you want to delete the whole word you can easily get to its beginning with a **b** command, so that does not matter very much.

4. The use of the **xp** sequence to correct transpositions is taken from *Introducing the UNIX System,* by Henry McGilton and Rachel Morgan. See App. F for a description of that book and of others on the UNIX system.

5. The double quote symbol, not a pair of single quotes.

Mastering vi!

What have you done so far? You have learned, as was promised in the Prologue to this part, how to move around the screen, add and remove text, move it from one place to another, and finally store it away safely when you are through. That is about 80 percent of all editing tasks.

Your next task is to master this material fully; that is, you should not need to think about the mechanics of editing while making any but the most complicated changes in your text. You should say to yourself "I want the text to be like this," and your fingers should make it happen.

One of the essential steps in achieving this flowing from the fingers is to develop a pattern for doing many of the most common tasks. If you want to move the cursor along the line you are on, you have the choice of moving with the arrowlike keys or the word keys, or searching for a suitable pattern. You must choose for yourself and consistently use a pattern, otherwise you will start thinking "How do I do this?" instead of just *doing* it.

While discussing working habits, let's return to the question of modes. This may give rise to some problems if you are not careful. These problems will not be serious if you are awake, but will waste time and make you think about the process of editing rather than about your text. They arise most often when you are inserting text and pause to think about what to do next. When you decide, you may not be sure whether you are in the insertion or command mode. When this happens, get out of the insertion mode as soon as you stop entering text. Also, before resuming insertion, give a second **ESC** to be absolutely sure that you are in the command mode; follow this with an **i** or **a** command, as appropriate. A related problem, mentioned in Chapter 4, is caused by giving partial commands and entering an operator without its operand. The next character entered will be taken as the operand, with potentially disastrous consequences. Here again, use the **ESC** key after any pause to be sure that partially entered commands are deleted.

In any case, listen for the bell! It is your best warning that something is wrong. Often it rings when you try to enter text while in the command mode. While almost all the alphabet is used for commands, some letters are not, and some combinations of letters give rise to inappropriate commands. However, owing to the frequency of the letters "a" and "i" in the English language, you may soon be in insertion mode, with half of your first word treated as commands. For example, if while in the command mode you try to enter the word *this,* the first two letters will be considered a command to position the cursor before the next letter "h" on that line; the "i" will be treated as an insert command, and your text will start in the middle of a word, with the final "s"!

PROLOGUE TO PART II

Ex Commands
in the Visual Mode

In Part I you have learned the basics of editing in the visual mode. The next step is to master it. The first step towards mastery is becoming proficient with the previous material. Furthermore, since the editor is normally used to enter material that will be processed under the UNIX system, you should begin to acquire at least some familiarity with the system. By now you should at least be comfortable with the concepts of files, directories, and commands given to the system.

The next step is to learn how to use certain **ex** commands in the visual mode. Such commands differ from those given to **vi** in three respects:

1. Commands start with a colon (:), while **vi** commands are not preceded by anything. The function of the initial colon is in fact to identify the command as being an **ex** one.

2. As soon as the colon is entered, it appears at the beginning of the last line of the screen, a line that is always kept clear for that purpose. In addition, the command appears on that line as it is being entered. You will recall that **vi** commands do not appear on the screen; the only thing you see is their effect.

3. Finally, the **ex** commands only become effective after you give a **CR** to signal that the command has been fully entered. That is the norm in the UNIX system (and almost all other computer systems). The **vi** editor's response to commands without needing a **CR** is the exception, not the rule.

Chapter 6 deals with many of the settable options used with the editor. Many of these options affect the use of the editor in the visual mode, but all are set in the **ex** mode. It also discusses features of **vi** that are specially useful when entering programs or continuous text. Logically, this material should be in Chap. 3, but as it is more advanced, it has been postponed. It deals with how to identify your terminal. If you have a system that works for you, and are not curious about what goes on, you will not need to read Sec. 6.2, which is probably more advanced than anything else in Part II.[1] The rest of Chap. 6 is straightforward; you should learn what options are available to you and experiment with them. You may well end up using the default values most of the time, but at least you will have made a choice.

Chapter 7 deals with file manipulation. Much of the time you will be using the simplest mode, editing a single file and exiting with a **ZZ** command. Almost all users need the more sophisticated methods more often than they realize; hence you should read that chapter carefully. At least you will know where to find out about file manipulation when you need to.

Finally, Chap. 8 deals with a variety of topics that do not fit in elsewhere. Any user of **vi** should be familiar with the search and substitute commands, while abbreviations and macros can often save a lot of time. Section 8.2 is certainly interesting; read it and file away the information for when you will need it.

Fewer examples are given than in Part I. This does not mean experimentation is any less important now, but that you should be able to construct your own examples. Also, continue reading the book at your terminal; it is certainly the most effective way to learn.

NOTES TO PART II

1. Not really more advanced in the sense of being harder to understand, but rather in the sense that most users do not learn about command files, especially of the **.login** or **.profile** variety, until a later stage in their UNIX experience.

6

Selecting Options

There are many options that the user of the **vi** editor can select. Three groups of options are described in this chapter: those related to screen management, text entry, and program entry. Those related to the reading and writing of files will be described in Chap. 7, while those that remain will be described in Chap. 8. Appendix C lists them all (with very brief descriptions). Several topics that seem closely related to option selection will also be discussed here.

6.1 GENERAL FEATURES

The **vi** editor is the screen-oriented component of a complex editor, **ex**. The setting of options is done from within the **ex** component of that editor. They are set through the **:set** command, usually abbreviated to **:se**. As noted in the Prologue to this part, **ex** commands differ from **vi** ones in three respects:

1. They start with a colon.
2. They are echoed on the bottom line of the screen.
3. They do not take effect until a **CR** has been entered. In Part I that **CR** was always explicitly shown; from now on it will be omitted.

All options have abbreviations that are used in practice. In the text the name is given in full, and the abbreviations are listed in the summaries at the chapter ends and in Appendix C. Several options, separated by spaces, can be given with a single **:se** command; hence individual option commands cannot have any embedded spaces. Specifically, options with an equals sign cannot have spaces on either side of the equals sign.

These options can be divided into three kinds. First there are the on/off options, which can take on only two values, on or off. They are also often called Boolean or toggle options. For example, if you want to use the autoindent feature you give the command

:se autoindent

while if you do not want it you give the command

:se noautoindent

The second type is the numerical valued options. An example is the tabstop option; should you want to set tab stops every four positions you would give the command

:se tabstop=4

Finally you have the string options. The most commonly used are those defining the paragraph and section macros, which define the beginnings of paragraphs for **vi**. For the **me** macros the section macros are **sh** and **uh**. Therefore use the command

:se sections=shuh

together with a similar one for paragraphs.

The command **:se** by itself will list the options that have settings other than the default, while **:se all** will list the current setting of all options (almost a whole screenful!).

To find the setting of a single numerical or string valued option, enter **:se** followed by the option name, thus

:se tabstop

will print the current value of the **tabstop** option. For the toggle options this will not work, since it would set the option. In that case the option name is followed by a **?**, so to find out whether **autoindent** is on or off, enter

:se autoindent?

These options, together with some other information for the editor, can be entered from the keyboard during an editing session. If you will always want to use a certain set of options you can store them, together with some other information, in a file called **.exrc** in your home directory (the directory you get into when you login). Note the period at the beginning of the file-name;[1] files with names starting with periods are "invisible" files which will normally not show up when you list the files in your directory.[2] To see them in a directory listing, give the command **ls -a** where **a** stands for "all."

6.2 IDENTIFYING YOUR TERMINAL

The **vi** editor needs to know two things about your terminal before it can start: what kind of terminal you are using, and at what rate it is communicating with the computer? The second item is easy to get from the operating system, which knows what speed you are communicating at. There are several ways in which you can tell the computer what kind of terminal you are using. If you always use the same kind of terminal, the easiest way is to put the name of your terminal (suitably abbreviated—ask someone at your installation) in your **.exrc** file:

:se term=vt100

if you are using a Digital Equipment Corporation VT100 terminal. If you use more than one kind of terminal (one at home and another at the office, or if you have access to a variety of public terminals) you will have to tell the computer each time you login which you are using. There are at least two different approaches to doing this. You can tell the computer what kind of terminal you are using before invoking **vi** (only once per login session), or you can modify your login procedure so that you are asked to enter the name of your terminal each time you login. Unfortunately, there are two different ways of implementing either approach, depending on whether you are using the classic Bell Laboratories (often called the Bourne) shell or the C shell developed at Berkeley.

Using the Bourne shell you can type

TERM = vt100; export TERM

at any time before invoking the **vi** editor. With the C shell you would enter

setenv TERM vt100

In both cases the capital letters are essential. As noted above, you only need to do this once per session.

To modify your login procedure you must make (or alter, if you already have one) a file whose name depends on which shell you are using. With the Bourne shell the file is called **.profile**; with the C shell it is called **.login**. Note in both cases the period at the start of the name; as we noted above such files are normally "invisible." With the Bourne shell you would create a file that contains

```
echo −n "enter tty type:"
read TERM
export TERM
echo "terminal type = " $ TERM
```

This sequence of four instructions will be executed whenever you login; it will result in the computer prompting you for the name of your terminal and storing that name where other programs can access it. It is not essential that you understand how this sequence of instructions works, but it will be explained in outline nevertheless. For further detail refer to any of the UNIX books described in App. F.

The first instruction,

echo −n "enter tty type:"

will display the phrase in quotes on your terminal. The **−n** preceding it is a modifier (usually called a flag) that prevents the normal carriage return after the message is printed. Try using the **echo** command both with and without the flag. First enter (when not in the editor!)

echo "Hello, World!"

The computer should print the phrase Hello World (without the quotation marks) and move to the next line, where it will give you the prompt. Now try

echo −n "Hello, World!"

You should get the same phrase, but this time the prompt will be on the same line as the message. Hence the first instruction in the little program above will print "enter tty type:" and wait for your response, which will appear on the same line. The second instruction will *read* the string you enter in response to the prompt (the name of your terminal) and put it in (assign it to, to use a more formal terminology) the variable TERM. The third instruction, **export TERM**, will make the value of that variable available to any program (including **vi**) that you run during the current session (until you logout). The fourth and final command prints out two things: the expression "terminal type = " (without quotes) and then the contents of the variable $TERM, which is the name of your terminal type.

Why have the computer print it out, since you know perfectly well what you entered? There is no real need, but it does give you a chance to detect an error.[3] It is considered good programming practice to always check that the computer interpreted your input correctly. If you are using the C shell, make a **.login** file that is very similar:

```
echo −n "enter tty type:"
setenv TERM $<
echo "terminal type = " $TERM
```

The instruction **setenv TERM $<** sets the environmental variable TERM to whatever you enter at the terminal, the expression **$<** being the C shell equivalent of **read**.

If your installation is running the full Berkeley version of UNIX, you might try to use the **tset** program, which can be "told" what kind of terminal is attached to each port. The instructions for using **tset** are very obscurely written; do not try to understand them unless you are an experienced computer user. If, however, you can get someone to write a suitable routine for you, it may well be the easiest way to tell the system what type of terminal you are using.

6.3 SCREEN MANAGEMENT

Keeping the screen synchronized with the computer's representation of your text takes time, so updating the screen is sometimes delayed. There are two kinds of costs involved: computing costs and time costs. The former depend on how "smart" your terminal is. Some terminals can make substantial changes to the display with minimal instructions from the computer; others need the computer to determine the placement of each character on the screen. The second cost depends on the speed of the communications link between your terminal and the computer; the slower the link the more time it takes for a given amount of information to go from the computer to your terminal.

6.3.1 Window Size

As a result, the amount of text which the computer keeps on your screen depends on the speed of your link. The number of lines the computer will initially put on your screen is called the "window size"; it is normally 8 lines with a communication rate of less than 1200 baud,[4] 16 lines for 1200 baud, and the whole screen less the last line for higher rates. You may want to change that default in either direction. Thus, though you use a slow link, you may be willing to wait a little longer to see more context around what you are editing. On the other hand, even with a fast link it takes time to redraw the whole screen, and if you are moving around a large file making minimal corrections you may well want a smaller window than the default. The change is made using the

:se window=n

command, which will set the window size to *n* lines. As noted above, this can be done during any session or, if you want a permanently different window size, by putting that command in your **.exrc** file.

There is an interesting variant on the window command which allows you to set different values for different speeds. This command is:

:se w300=n*

and similar commands are **w1200*** and **w9600.*** They allow you to set your own defaults for slow (below 1200 baud), intermediate (1200 baud), or high-speed (above 1200 baud) terminals. This is useful if you use more than one terminal, such as a fast terminal at work and a slower one, communicating over telephone lines, at home.

6.3.2 Scrolling Parameters

The number of lines scrolled after a **Control–D** or **Control–U** instruction also depends on the speed of your terminal, or rather on your window size. Normally it is set at half the current window size, whether that is the normal default size or one

---

*This command is not present in all versions of the editor. Throughout this book, all commands (whether editor or UNIX) that may be absent, or function differently, on certain systems will be marked with an asterisk. These differences will be discussed in App. E.

selected by you. It is less easy to change than any of the other options; setting the **scroll** parameter works only in the **ex** mode. However, it is possible to change it during the current session by entering *n***Control–D**. This will scroll *n* lines and, more to the point, reset the effective scroll parameter to that number of lines until changed. Unfortunately there is no easy way to put this in your **.exrc** file.

I do not use the default values of either the window or scroll parameters because it takes time to update the screen when I move around with a large window, and, while entering text, I do not specially care how much of it is visible on the screen. Thus I use a fairly small window (currently eight lines). On the other hand, I often use scroll to get a global idea of what I have entered, and find that half of that window size is too little. Therefore I give a **12Control–D** command as soon as I start editing a file on a reasonably fast (1200 or faster) terminal, and use a **8Control–D** when using a 300 baud[5] terminal.

6.3.3 Other Display Options and Commands

There are three options that affect the way in which the computer tries to keep the screen updated. The first is the **optimize** option, which should always be set. It abolishes the carriage return at the end of each line when printing multiple lines, speeding output on dumb terminals when printing lines with leading white space (blanks or tabs). There is no reason to change it.

The second deals with the way in which the terminal display is updated during insertions. If **slowopen** is on, the screen will not be updated during insertions on most terminals; when **noslowopen** is on, an attempt is made (not always successfully!) to update the screen during insertions. Note that if the computer has to do the updating (rather than a very smart terminal doing it on its own), substantial amounts of computing time may be consumed. Try both and see what you get!

Finally there is the **redraw** option, which will force the computer to redraw the screen (or at least the current line) after each character insertion. Do not use this; it is only useful at high speeds on lightly loaded computers.

You saw above that **INT** will stop the updating of the display and may leave your screen in a mess. There are a pair of commands that can help here. The basic command is **Control–L** (linefeed will do the same on terminals with such a key), which will redraw the screen the way it "should" look. A very similar command is **Control–R**, which will redraw the screen and specifically close up gaps left after deleting lines (you will recall that on many terminals deleted lines are replaced by @ acting as a placeholder).

One of the things that can mess up your screen is receiving a message while you are editing. UNIX has a facility, called **write**[6], which allows users to send messages to each other. Normally a parameter is set to **mesg**, allowing you to receive messages. You can, if you wish, prevent such messages from reaching you by using **:se nomesg***. However, the inconvenience of an occasionally messed up screen is a small price to pay for the ability to communicate with other users.

A not very useful command, **z**, should probably be mentioned here. It will lead to the redrawing of the screen in a way that depends on the character that follows it. Thus **zCR** will redraw the screen with the current line at the top, **z–** with the current line at the bottom, and **z.** with the current line in the middle of the screen.

6.4 OPTIONS AND COMMANDS FOR PROGRAM ENTRY

There are several options which make program entry easier. The most important are a set which help indent programs properly. Current programming practice strongly encourages the indentation of source programs to help show their structure. There are editors that can "understand" your program and indent it appropriately. The **vi** editor is not quite smart enough to do so, but with the **autoindent** option it will indent each line to the same level as the previous line, whether you have used spaces or tabs; in insertion mode, whenever you hit a **CR** at the end of a line, or open up a new line with **o** or **O**, the cursor will start under the first non-blank character on the previous line. To increase the level of indentation, start the line with a further tab. Decreasing the level of indentation is not so intuitively obvious, as you cannot back-space over the tabs with your erase character. A **Control–D**, however, will back you up one indentation level, and reset the indentation level there.

There are also commands that can temporarily reset your indentation level to zero for the current line (**^Control–D**), returning to the old level on the next, or reset it without returning to the old level (**0Control–d**).

The system normally sets the tab stops every 8 positions, and that is often a convenient place to put them. If, however, your program is deeply indented, or if you use an older terminal (or personal computer) with a narrow screen, you may wish to have the tabs set at smaller distances. This is not a really suitable approach, as the new tab settings will only have an effect during the editing session. If you then list the program on a printer, it will use the normal tab settings. In many cases, material that was nicely aligned using the editor becomes unaligned on printing.

To put them on every fourth position use

   :se tabstop = 4 shiftwidth = 4

The first command will make the screen display routines expand the tabs to every fourth position, while the second will make **Control–D** backspace over four positions.

A more suitable approach is to use **Control–T** instead of the tab key to indent. You can use the **:se shiftwidth =** n command to set the number of spaces it will indent (default is eight). It is a smart command, and will insert a combination of tabs and spaces to get you to where you want to be. If you are very used to the tab key, you can use the **:map!** command (Sec. 8.3.1) to translate tabs into **Control–T**s:

   :map! tab Control–T

where the tab key is pressed rather than entering the letters t, a, b, and similarly for **Control–T**.

There is a similar command that allows you to change the level of indentation of a program which has already been entered. Supposing you decide that you want to loop round a set of lines that were initially only going to be executed once. You will now have to indent these lines one level more. It would not be too difficult to add a tab to each, but there is an indent operator, **>**, that will indent each line of an object by one shiftwidth. In common with most other operators, doubling it (**>>**) will make it act on the current line. Obviously **3>>** will indent three lines, and **>3L** will indent lines till the third from the bottom of the current screen. The opposite operator, as you should have guessed, is **<**, which will shift lines one level to the left. Note that it behaves sanely; if your text is unindented and you give it a **<<** command, you will not lose the leading text.

There are a pair of other options that are very useful during program entry. The first of these is **showmatch**. With it on, whenever you type a right parenthesis or brace, the cursor will move for about one second to the corresponding (or balancing) left object if it is on the screen. If there is no corresponding unmatched parenthesis, the terminal will beep at you. This is, of course, absolutely essential for those entering programs in the programming language lisp; it is extremely useful even for less parenthesized languages such as C. Similar to it is a command, **%**, which works whether or not the showmatch option is set. If this command is given with the cursor on a parenthesis, brace, or bracket, the cursor will move to the corresponding (balancing) object. It is very useful when checking a program before compiling it.

The other option is for lisp users, and is appropriately called **lisp***. When it is on, especially in conjunction with autoindent, it formats programs in the lisp tradition, with open lists suitably lined up and indented. The command **=*** given after a lisp program has been entered will realign material as if it had been entered with the **lisp** and **autoindent** options set. If you are a lisp programmer, try entering a program without setting these two options and without aligning the program manually. Then move the cursor to the start of a function and enter **=%**. Do you understand the structure of this command? The **=** is an operator, and the **%** tells it to act until the balancing parenthesis. Furthermore, the commands **(**, **{**, and their inverses move over s–expressions, the difference being that **{** does not move over atoms.

There is another feature that is extremely useful to programmers maintaining large programs contained in several files, namely the **tag** command. Since it deals with files it will be discussed in Chap. 7.

6.5 OPTIONS AND COMMANDS FOR TEXT ENTRY

Just as there are a variety of options and commands that make life easier for those entering programs, there are several features that make the entry of straight text much easier and more pleasant.

Perhaps the most important of these features by far is the **wrapmargin*** option. With that option on, whenever the current line on the screen comes within a certain distance of the right margin, the word being entered is moved automatically to the next line. The numeric argument to this option sets the boundary across which text is not allowed to pass; thus specifying

> **:se wrapmargin=8**

means that no text will be allowed beyond eight columns from the right margin of your screen[7], i.e., a maximum line length of 72 characters if your screen has the normal 80 character width.

This option is invaluable for two reasons. First it frees you from having to think about carriage returns while entering text (the computer remembers such things better than you do!). Secondly, it gives the entered text a nice appearance, and even though it will be processed by a formatter before appearing on paper it does make it much nicer to read and revise on the screen.

This brings up a related point. After the text has been entered it will be revised, often extensively. If you insert text at the beginning of a line, the line may become very long. Should you now split it (remember how? if not see section 4.3.2!) you will have two short lines. In any case, deleting a phrase will shorten other lines considerably. Should a paragraph get too ragged, it is possible to smooth it out (at a cost!). Enter {. That will get you to the start of the current paragraph (how paragraphs are delimited will be defined in a moment). Now enter **!}fmt***.

The explanation of this command really belongs in Sec. 8.2.1; it is included here because it is so closely related to the **wrap-margin** option. If you do not understand how it works, return to it after Chap. 8. The **!** command takes two arguments. The first is an object, in this case text through the end of the current paragraph. That object is then handed to the second argument, which is a UNIX command that takes the text given to it as input and puts its output where that text was. The command **fmt** is a moderately smart formatter that will even text out to lines of about 72 characters each, and is smart enough to leave lines that start with a period (commands to the real formatters) unchanged. If you want, go to the top of the file with a **1G** command, then give a **!Gfmt** command; this will format the whole file. In most cases this would be very unwise. Most files will contain some text that you want to keep as is, delimited by **.nf** and **.fi** commands to the formatter. These commands will be ignored by **fmt,** leading to a mess that will have to be cleaned up.

When discussing paragraphs in Chap. 4, we noted that exactly what paragraph delimiters were depends on the particular set of word processing macros you are using. There are currently three commonly used sets of macros on most UNIX systems: the **ms** and **mm** macros developed at Bell Laboratories and the **me** macros developed at Berkeley. The default set assumed by **vi** varies from version to version, and you should use the **:se all** command to see what the default symbols are. If these are the same as those you use, you need do nothing. Otherwise you will have to tell the editor what symbols you use to refer to paragraphs of various kinds.

Since instructions to the formatter always start with a period in column 1, you do not have to put that period in your definition as given to the editor. You do, however, have to give all the one or two letter combinations that can produce a paragraph. With the **me** macros **pp** will produce an ordinary paragraph, **ip** will produce an indented paragraph, **np** will produce a numbered paragraph, and **lp** will produce a left justified paragraph. Hence the user of **me** macros should give a set command for paragraphs of

    :se paragraphs = ppipnplp

Similarly the sections are defined by

    :se sect=shuh

where **sh** and **uh** give numbered and unnumbered section headings respectively.

6.6 ENTERING CONTROL CHARACTERS

The **beautify** option will cause the editor to reject control characters (except for **CR**[8] and **tab**) during input. This avoids entering control characters into files if you accidentally use the control key instead of the shift key. The default is **nobeautify**; you should use it as it simplifies the entering of abbreviations and macros (Sec. 8.3).

    Should you want to enter a control character into a file while using the **beautify** option, precede it immediately by **Control–V**. As soon as you enter the **Control–V** you will get a caret (^) on the screen, and if you now enter the control character you want it will appear on the screen as a capital immediately after the caret.[9] The combination **^X** is the way **vi** shows control characters on the screen;[10] it represents a single character, not two.

6.7 SUMMARY OF NEW COMMANDS AND OPTIONS

The following new commands were introduced in this chapter. The first group acts during insertion mode and the second during command mode. Those marked with an asterisk are not found in all versions of the editor.

Control-D	back up over one level of indentation if autoindent set (6.4)
0Control-D	kill autoindent (6.4)
^Control-D	kill autoindent on this line, restore it on next (6.4)
Control-T	if in autoindent mode, insert one **shiftwidth** blank or tab c)6.4)

Control-L	redraw screen, useful if scrambled (6.3.3)
Control-R	redraw screen, eliminating deleted lines marked by @ (6.3.3)
%	if given with cursor on (, { or [, moves it to matching), } or] (6.4)
<	decrease indent of each level of object by one shiftwidth (6.4)
=*	reindent lisp program, as if it had been entered using lisp and auto-indent options (6.4)
>	indent each line of object by one more shiftwidth (6.4)
z	redraw screen around current line (6.3.3)

The following options, each followed by its abbreviated name and default in parentheses, were introduced in this chapter:

:se autoindent	(ai, noai) set autoindentation feature (6.4)
:se beautify	(bf, nobf) prevent entry of control characters (6.6)
:se lisp*	(lisp, nolisp) autoindent indents appropriately for lisp, and (), {} and [] commands suitably redefined (6.4)
:se mesg*	(mesg, mesg) allow messages to be received (6.3.3)
:se optimize	(opt, noopt) apolishes automatic **CR** when terminal prints (6.3.3)
:se paragraphs=*xxxx*	(para, para=IPLPPPQPP LIbp) specifies paragraph macros used by { and } commands (6.5)
:se redraw	(redraw, noredraw) simulate intelligent terminal on dumb one (6.3.3)
:se scroll=*n*	(scroll, scroll=½ window) set scrolling parameter to *n* lines (**ex** only) (6.3.2)

:se sections=*xxxx*	(sections, sections=SHNHH HU) specifies section macros used by [[and]] commands (6.5)
:se shiftwidth=*n*	(sw, s=8) number of characters to be backspaced over by Control–D when autoindent is on (6.4)
:se showmatch	(sm, nosm) when) or } is entered, move cursor for one second to matching (or { (6.4)
:se slowopen	(slow, terminal dependent) delays updating of screen during insertions (6.3.3)
:se tabstop=*n*	(ts, ts=8) set editor tabs every *n* characters (6.4)
:se w300=*n**	set window size to *n* lines if speed is 300 baud (6.3.1)
:se window=*n*	(window, speed dependent) set window size to *n* lines (6.3.1)
:se wrapmargin=*n**	(wm, wm=0) set margin for word wraparound at *n* characters from end of line (6.5)

NOTES TO CHAPTER 6

1. Follow the universal UNIX practice of referring to the name of a file (in a generic way) as its filename.

2. Nor will they be included in most commands that refer to groups of files using the so–called wildcard specifications. They are very unobtrusive files that will not make their presence known unless you go out of your way to inquire about them. The reason is that they tend to be very static, doing their job quietly.

3. If you do detect an error, you can logout and repeat your login sequence. Alternatively, you can re–run the **.profile** program by entering **sh .profile** and giving the correct terminal type.

4. While the term "baud" has a rather complex technical definition, it is adequate to think of it as "bits per second." Dividing by ten will give an excellent estimate of the number of characters per second transmitted.

5. The solution to the problems of using **vi** with slow communication lines is to not use them! With the decrease in the prices of minimal 1200 baud modems, communication at 300 baud is rapidly becoming obsolete.

6. **Write** is a very useful command; look it up in the UNIX programmer's manual or any book on UNIX that you may have (see App. F for suggested reading).

7. The command **:se wrapmargin = 0** disables the wrapmargin option. It is the default.

8. Together with newline and linefeed.

9. This will work exactly the same way even if you are not using the **beautify** option, except that in the latter case you can enter it directly.

10. It is also the method used in the **vi** documentation; I have preferred the explicit representation **Control–X** here.

7

File Manipulation

In this chapter you will learn how to use files in a more sophisticated way than you learned in Part I. This will require a bit more knowledge of the UNIX system than you have needed so far.

7.1 SIMPLE EDITING

In the simplest (and commonest) case you do not explicitly read or write any files. This does not mean that no reading or writing of files takes place, but that it is done for you. When you enter, at the UNIX level, the command **vi myfile** one of two things happens. If the file already exists, it is read into the editor's buffer and is ready to be edited. If it does not exist, a new file is created with that name. That new file is initially empty, and the system informs you that a new file is being created. Should you exit the editing session without writing out a newly created file, it will be quietly removed.

There are several reasons for getting a message that a new

file is being created when you thought you were editing an existing one. The commonest is a misspelled file name, or a missing extension (the symbol after the dot in the filename). Thus to edit an existing file called **myfile.c** enter either **vi myfile** or **vi mifile.c** and the "new file" message will be produced. The UNIX command **ls** will give you a list of your files, and you can check the spelling. A second reason is that you are not in the directory that you think you are in. The command **pwd** will print the directory you are currently in (it stands for print working directory). The third reason, fortunately a rare one, is that someone (you?) has removed the file. If that has happened, see the system administrator before despairing. A backup copy of your file, or at least of a recent version of it, will probably exist if the file is more than a day old.

Once the editor has a file name, it remembers it; any explicit or implicit write command will be to that file, unless another file is explicitly named. In the simplest of cases you only give one implicit write command as part of the **ZZ** command to exit. The editor also remembers whether you have made any modifications to a file since you last wrote it. If you have made no modifications since it was last written, the **ZZ** command will exit without writing. Why would you not make modifications? You may want just to look at the file to see whether in fact you did correct an error you had previously noted. Alternately, you may have been writing the buffer into the file periodically as you went along.

In the past it was considered wise to write out the contents of the buffer periodically, so that in the event of a system crash or a telephone line disconnection your work would not be lost. One of the many improvements in **vi/ex** is the ability to recover files that were being edited when the system crashed or the telephone connection was lost.

7.2 RECOVERING FROM HANGUPS AND CRASHES

You noted in Sec. 2.5 that your file does not get modified during an editing session; all changes take place in a temporary copy, often referred to as the buffer. At the end of a normal session, this buffer is copied (written) into your permanent file unless you instruct the editor to end the session without saving the modified file. What happens if the computer malfunctions (crashes is the usual term) while you are editing, or if your telephone connection gets disconnected? With many older editors the entire editing session would be lost; hence the suggestion that the buffer be frequently written to permanent storage.

The **vi/ex** system has provisions for saving the buffer when a session terminates abnormally; only a few lines of editing (if any) are lost. This is usually saved in a directory called **/tmp**, though the details need not concern you. When you next log on you will get a message from the system (via **mail**) warning you that you have a "lost" file. To demonstrate how this works, I hung up the phone while editing this file. Logging on again I got the message "You have mail" and on giving the **mail** command[1] I got the following message:

> A copy of an editor buffer of your file "chap7"
> was saved when the editor was killed.
> This buffer can be retrieved using the "recover" command of
> the editor.
> An easy way to do this is to give the command "ex -r chap7".
> This works for "edit" and "vi" also.

The command **vi -r chap7** recovered the file for me with all the changes I had made.

7.3 WRITING AND READING FILES

The basic commands for writing and reading files are the **ex** commands **:w** and **:r**.

7.3.1 The Write Command

The basic write command (the only one considered in this chapter) writes all or part of the contents of the buffer into a file. Note that if you used the methods of editing advocated in this book, a filename would always be associated with your buffer. When editing an already existing file, the name of that file is associated with the buffer. Furthermore, all examples of file creation have been of the form

vi *filename*

so the buffer's contents are, from the very start, associated with a filename. It is possible, though rarely appropriate, to start an editing session with a simple **vi** command. In that case the buffer's contents will not be associated with any filename, and a **Control–G** command (Sec. 4.4.1) will reveal that it has no name. A filename can be associated with it by giving the command

:f *filename*

(the command **:f** alone shows the current state of the file, like **Control–G**).

The fundamental, unadorned write command (**:w**) will write out the contents of the buffer into the associated file. A very simple extension,

:w *filename*

will write the contents of the buffer into *filename*, destroying its contents if it exists.[2] Finally, if the command is preceded by a pair of line numbers separated by a comma, only the lines within that range will be written. Thus the full–fledged command

:8,17w junk

will write lines eight to 17 of the current buffer into the file **junk**.

As pointed out in Sec. 4.4.1, line numbers are not a very good tool to use. You will see below that there are several other ways of referring to a range of lines to be written out to a file.

A variant of the write command exists that appends the current buffer to the end of the file it is written to. It is a variation on a UNIX command, **>>**, that appends output to the end of a file. The **ex** command

:w >> *filename*

will append the contents of the buffer to the end of *filename*.

7.3.2 The Read Command

The basic read command reads the contents of the named file into the current editor buffer, placing them after the line on which the cursor was when the command was given:

> **:r** *filename*

If you give a line number (or surrogate) before the command, the contents of the file will be placed after the line referred to:

> **:5r** *filename*

will put the contents of *filename* in the buffer after line five. How can you put the contents of that file *before* the first line in your buffer? While there is no line numbered zero, the command

> **:0r** *filename*

will put the contents before line one.

7.4 CUT AND PASTE EDITING

The expression "cut and paste editing" is often used to describe the moving of text from one part of a file to another, using deletes or yanks followed by puts, as described in Chap. 4. Here you will learn how to move chunks of text from one file to another. This can be very useful if you are writing a pair of related articles and the first article has a paragraph that you would like to copy into the second one, to use either unchanged or with minor changes. Another example is writing a book and keeping each chapter in a separate file (as I am doing right now!). You may decide that something in Chap. 5 (kept in a file called, appropriately enough, chap5) really belongs in Chap. 8.

As an example, use the file **decl** that you have been using all along. Suppose that you are writing a paper and want to quote the second paragraph of the Declaration of Independence in full. You could obviously retype it, but the whole idea of using computers to enter text is to minimize such retyping.

Let's say that the final product you want is the one shown in Fig. 7–1, and that you want it in a file called **paper**; there are several approaches (some better than others) that you can take.

If you have not yet entered the text of **paper**, there is a very simple way. First copy the entire file **decl** into **paper** with the command

cp decl paper

Now edit **paper** (which is a copy of **decl**) and remove the lines that you do not want. The simplest way is to get to the blank line before the section you want to keep (using **}** to get there) and delete all lines from the start up to that section (using **d1G**). Use a second **}** to get to the blank line after that paragraph, and delete from it to

> This is a very learned paper commenting on the many and, indeed, numerous insights to be found within the confines of the second paragraph of the Declaration of Independence:
>
> We hold these truths to be selfevident, that all men are created equal, that they are endowed by their creator with certain unalienable rights, that among these are Life, Liberty and the pursuit of Happiness. That to secure these rights, Governments are instituted among men, deriving their just powers from the consent of the governed. That whenever any Form of Government becomes destructive of these ends, it is the right of the People to alter or abolish it, and to institute new Government, laying its foundation on such principles and organizing its powers in such form, as to them shall seem most likely to effect their Safety and Happiness.
>
> A careful perusal of this document cannot fail to impress us with the great wisdom and insight of this Nation's Founding Fathers.

Fig. 7–1: The composite document we are trying to produce.

the end of the file with a **dG** command. You now have a file containing those lines of the Declaration of Independence that you want, and can add your text above and below them. This is not really what is meant by "cut and paste editing."

A more interesting situation and a genuine "cut and paste editing" job would occur if you had already written the material you wanted in **paper** except for the extract from the Declaration of Independence.

There are two distinct approaches to doing the job. The first is to get the lines of text that you want to copy into a file that you will call **common**, as it contains lines of text common to **decl** and **paper**. This file is then read into **paper** in the appropriate place. The second approach involves the sequential editing of files; this approach will be described in the next two sections.

To start off, edit the file **paper** containing the first four and last three lines of the final product, i.e., those that are not to be taken from **decl**. You will then produce **common** in several ways, and read it into **paper**.

One way of making **common** is first to copy all of **decl** into **common**; the command

cp decl common

will do so. Now edit **common** and remove all material preceding and following the part you want to keep, as described above. Only the lines you want remain in the buffer; save them and exit the editor with a **ZZ** command.

Getting these lines into **paper** is simple; edit it, move the cursor to the fourth line, and give the command **:r common** which will read the file **common** and put it into the buffer below the position of the cursor. Now add blank lines above and below the copied text and you are through; exit with a **ZZ** command and delete the now useless file **common**.

There are at least two other ways of producing the file **common**.[3] The first is dangerous, and is given both to illustrate a point and to warn against its use. Edit **decl** and, as in the first method, remove the unwanted lines. Next give the command **:w common** to write the remaining text into **common**, and follow this by a **:q** command to take you out of the editor. The point of this method is to show you that you do not have to write back into the file that you had initially edited but can write the buffer into any file.

What is the danger? What would happen if, instead of **:w**

common you just entered **:w?** You would have written your truncated version of **decl** over the original and lost it! It is very dangerous to take a file that you want to keep, cut it up, and write the remainder elsewhere. It costs nothing to first copy it into the file in which you will want to put the remainder, and cut it up there.

The last method involves writing out only part of the buffer to a file. So far all our write commands, implicit or explicit, have written out the entire buffer. Edit **decl** and move the cursor to the first line you want to save in **common**. Give a **Control–G** command; it will tell you that you are on line 16 of the file. Then go to the last common line and repeat the **Control–G** command, which will tell you that you are now on line 29. You want to write lines 16 to 29 into **common**, and rather than delete everything else and then write the file you can simply specify the range of lines you want to write out. The command **:16,29w common** will write lines 16 to 29 into **common**. Note that you first have the colon, which signals that it is an **ex** command, and then the range of lines to be acted on; then you have the command, and finally the file into which the lines are to be put.

What would have happened had you forgotten to enter the file name and just entered **:16,29w?** As you may guess, the material would have been written back into **decl**, destroying the original contents. Since the original contents are still in the buffer the damage is limited, and could be repaired by a simple **:w** followed by the correct **:16,29w common.**

You noted earlier that the use of line numbers is not the best way of identifying lines. There are several other ways of identifying lines when using **ex** commands. You already know one: the use of marks established using the **m** command. Mark the first line you want to write into **common** with a **ma** command, and similarly mark the last line with a **mb** command. Then, instead of using a range of line numbers, you could simply give the command

    :'a,'bw common

Is there still a simpler way? If you want to delete that range of lines and the cursor is on the last line to be deleted, give the **vi** command **'ad** and **vi** would delete text from the line on which the cursor is to the line marked **a**. Is there a way in which **ex** can use the fact that you want to write out lines from the one marked **a** to the one the cursor is[4] on? There is, and the concept of the **current line** is as important in **ex** as it is in **vi**. When in **vi**, the line which the cursor was on before an **ex** command was issued is the current line as far as **ex** is concerned. The current line can be referred to as **.**, usually referred to by **ex** or **ed** users as **dot**.

Hence in this example it would be sufficient for you to move to the first line you want to write, mark it as described, and then move to the last line to be written and give the command

    :'a,.w common

This will write lines, from the one marked **a** to the current line, into **common**.

7.5 EDITING FILES SUCCESSIVELY

So far you have been editing multiple files one at a time and exiting the editor after each editing job, even if you planned to re–enter it immediately. There is no need to do so, as giving the command **:vi** *filename* from within **vi** (or rather from **ex**, since it is a colon command) will have the same effect. That is to say the contents of the buffer will be replaced by the file *filename*. If you have made modifications to the original file and have not written it back you will get a warning message: "No write since last change (:visual! overrides)" or something similar. Should you not want to write the modified file back, you can use **vi!** *filename*. In the more common case in which you do want to keep the changes made, you would give a write command, followed by a second **:vi** *filename*.

It is not necessary to repeat *filename*; the command **:vi #** will have the same effect. How does it work? The **ex** editor maintains the names of two files. The first is the **current filename**, which is the name of the file currently being edited. It can be referred to as **%**, and an example of this usage is the spelling checking command sequence shown in Sec. 8.3.2. If a new value is given to the current filename, as is done when a **:vi** *filename* command is executed successfully, the previous current filename is stored as the **alternate filename**. Similarly, if a file is mentioned but does not become the current file, as happens when you try to edit a new file without having written the old one back, its name becomes the alternate filename. The alternate filename can be referred to as **#**; hence **:vi #** will edit the file that you tried to edit. This can even be shortened to a single **vi** command: **Control–.** [5]

This may appear to be similar to editing a file and then quitting, but it is not. The named buffers (see Chap. 4 if you have forgotten about them) are unchanged by changing the file being edited, while they are lost if you leave the editor.[6] This gives you yet another way of taking the common lines out of **decl** and putting them into paper. Edit **decl**, get the cursor on the first common line, and mark it with an **a**. Then get to the last common line and give the command **"ay'a**. This will yank the common lines into labeled buffer **a**.[7] Now give the command **vi paper**. There is no need to write **decl** back as it has not been modified. When **paper** is read in, go to the place where you want to put the common lines, and put them there with a **"ap** command.

Note that **decl** has now become the alternate filename; should you decide that you need a second quotation from it you can give the following pair of instructions:

```
:w
:vi #
```

This brings us to the subject of editing multiple files.

7.6 EDITING MULTIPLE FILES

One of the most powerful features of the **vi/ex** editor is its ability to edit multiple files. In the previous section you saw how you could edit several files in succession without leaving the editor; however, as far as each individual file is concerned, you are through with it after you start working on the next one. There are times when it is very convenient to switch back and forth between a series of related files.

For example, you may want to refer to one file while working on another; you may have the output of some computations in one file, and be editing a second file which contains a report on those results. You will often want to go from the report file to the results file, and you may also want to go to the program file (or files) to be sure that you know what the results really mean.

A second kind of situation arises when you want to do the same thing to a series of files. For example, after I had written about half of this book I received an author's guide from Prentice–Hall. One of the changes I had to make was in the way I had been referring to chapters. I had been spelling the word out in full, with the first letter in upper case. Prentice-Hall wanted the word spelled out in full only if it started a sentence, otherwise it had to be abbreviated to "Chap." with an upper case "C". It was simpler to edit all the files simultaneously than to go through each one separately.

Let's return to the example of copying a paragraph from **decl** into **paper**. Give the command

vi decl paper

The first message that you get, even before the screen clears, is

two files to edit

after which the screen clears, as usual, and you get the message

"decl", 37 lines, 1468 characters

To find out what files are being edited, you can give the command

:arg

where **arg** is short for arguments, and the list of files to edit is being considered arguments to the **vi** program. You will get

[decl] paper

with the file currently being edited in brackets. Now yank the lines you want to copy as before. To get to **paper** you now have only to give the command **:n** (for next). The effect is the same as if you had given the command

   :vi paper

The screen is first cleared and then **paper** appears. Now giving the **:arg** command will give

   decl [paper]

showing that **paper** is the file now being edited. What will happen if you give one more **:n** command? Not unexpectedly you will get a message

   no more files to edit

since you have edited all the files on your list. Should you want to go back to **decl** you would give the command **:rew** (for rewind); that will return you to your last position in **decl** before you moved from it to **paper**.

   If you modify the file you are editing and want to keep your changes, you must give a **:w** command before the **:n** command. If you do not you will get a

   no write since last change, n! overrides

message.[8]

   Finally, you can edit a completely new and unrelated set of files, without ever quitting **vi**, by giving the command

   :n *filelist*

where **filelist** is any explicit or implicit[9] list of filenames. Interestingly enough, it is not possible to give, while in **vi**, the command

   :vi *filelist*

to edit a list of files. While in **vi** the command **:vi** can only take a single filename as argument.

7.7 EDITING LARGE PROGRAMS

Current ideas of good programming practice suggest that large programs be broken down into smaller functional units (functions, subroutines, or procedures, depending on the language), which are often contained in several separate files.

Suppose that you have such a large program that you want to make changes in the function **myfunc**. First you must remember which file it is in. This may not be too difficult, but it is certainly something the computer should be able to do better than you. Even after you remember which file it is in, the problem of finding it remains. Searching with /**myfunc** is likely to turn up a large number of lines that look like this:

    y = myfunc (x, z);

They are not what you need. Fortunately there is a command that, with some preparation on your part, can find the definition of a function immediately. If you have a suitable database (and you will see below how to make one) the command

    :ta myfunc

where **:ta*** is short for tag, will get you into the correct file and position your cursor on the first (defining) line of **myfunc**. What will happen if **myfunc** is in another file and you have made changes to the current one?[10] As usual, you will get a warning message, and **:ta!** will get you out. In the more usual case, you will write out your file. You do not need to reenter **myfunc**; a second **:ta** command will search for the function named in the previous command.

A very interesting variation on this exists. Suppose you are editing a program, find the line

    y = weird (a, b, c)

---

*This command is not present in all versions of the editor. Throughout this book, all commands (whether editor or UNIX) that may be absent, or function differently, on certain systems will be marked with an asterisk. These differences will be discussed in App. E.

and have no idea of what "weird" does. You could obviously get to it by giving the command

:ta weird

A slightly simpler way is to get your cursor on the first letter of **weird** and give the command **Control–]***.

So far, nothing has been said about how to make the database needed by the **:ta** command. While it is possible to make it yourself, there is a command in the Berkeley system that will make it for you. Simply giving (at the UNIX level) the command*

ctags *filelist*

will create a file, called tags, with the required information on all functions in all files in *filelist*. If you are programming in C, the command

ctags *.c

will put the names of all functions in all C programs in your current directory into the tags file.

There is a pair of not very useful options related to the **:ta** command. The first is*:

:se taglength = *x*

which allows only the first *x* characters of the tag to be considered. A value of zero (the default) makes them all significant. The second option is*:

:se tags = *path of files*

The default is the file named **tags** in the current directory, and in most cases this is the most appropriate value.

If you do serious programming, use the tagging capability regularly. It, together with the UNIX programs **make** and the symbolic debuggers (**sdb** or **dbx**), greatly simplify the writing of large programs. See also Sec. 8.2.4 for the **error** program and for the use of **Control–Z** to suspend an editing session. **Make is** available on all UNIX systems, while the other programs mentioned here are only available in certain implementations.

7.8 PROTECTIONS

The UNIX file protection system divides users of a given file into three categories. The first is the owner of the file, normally the person who created that file in a directory under his account. Normally the owner can read and write to his files, modifying or removing them. He can, should he so desire, make a given file non–writable even by himself, and that is a way of avoiding the disaster of accidentally removing or overwriting an important file. However, it is rarely used, as UNIX users are supposed to know what they are doing, and in any case the system has adequate backup facilities. Normally a user can read and write all of his files.

The second main group consists of all other users. Systems differ; in a research environment with no classified work it is usual to allow all users to read all files unless their owners have specifically denied permission to read them. In other environments a stricter security system may be enforced, with the default being unreadable files. In any case permission to write to other people's files is normally denied.

In a few cases there is a third category of user; members of the same group may have separate accounts, but be allowed to read and perhaps write files in each other's directories.

These permissions are administered by the system, though a user may change the permissions on his files. Obviously, he cannot give himself permission to read or write another user's files.

The **vi/ex** editor offers some additional protection for one's files. Go back to the example in which you edited **decl** and wrote the remains of it into **common**. As noted at the time, the danger of this approach is that you might well have written it back into **decl**, destroying that file. To avoid the possibility you could have edited in the read only mode. As the name indicates, you can only read from the file you are editing and cannot write back into it. You can, however, write into another file. To edit in the read only mode, give the command **vi –R decl**. The **–R**[11] is called a command-line flag. Most UNIX commands take flags which modify them in one way or another. To see exactly what this does, give the command **vi –R decl**.[12] Instead of the usual message you will get something that says "decl read only" or something similar. Now try to give a **:w** command. You will get a message "decl read only" or words to that effect. Give the command **:w decl.new** and it will create a new file with that name, showing that "read only" applies to the original file being edited, not to the editing process. You can, should you decide to do so, write back into **decl**. To do that you must give the command **:w!** where the exclamation mark indicates that you want to over-ride the normal response to that command. You will note that this is similar to the **:q!** command discussed at the end of Chap. 2.

There is another aspect of protection. You may recall that you deleted the file **common** after you first created it. The reason was that normally the editor will only write to the file it is editing (unless the –R flag was used) or to a new file. If you have a **common** file left over from your experimentation, edit **decl** and try to give the command **:w16,29 common**. You will receive a message saying that the file already exists. If you replace the **:w** command by **:w!** the editor will execute it.[13]

7.9 FILE-RELATED OPTIONS

There are two important options related to file management; **autowrite** and **writeany**. The default is for both to be off, but you might well be better off with both of them on.

7.9.1 Autowrite

There are several commands that either cause you to exit the editor or to read in new files, and in either case you lose the current contents of your buffer if they have been modified since the last time you wrote them out. Normally the editor refuses to execute these commands unless you indicate that you know what you are doing by giving a **!** after the command.

You may well ask why the editor does not automatically write out the current file and get on with the job. The reason is that if you have made changes that you do not want to keep (i.e., have messed up the file) it should not be written back; this would destroy the unmessed original. This makes sense, and it would be unfortunate if in response to the command **:q** the editor wrote out your file.

There are, however, a few commands for which it seems to make sense to write out the buffer automatically. These are the commands in which you switch from one file to another: **:next, :rewind,** and **:tag.** In these cases, the autowrite option allows you to give a single command rather than two (write followed by whatever command you planned to give).

Also, as you will see in the next chapter, commands to the system can be given while in the editor. Such commands often deal with the current file, and if the version available to the system is not up-to-date, the results can be confusing, to say the least. For example, while writing a paper, you may wish to know how many words it contains. If the paper is in a file called **paper** the command would be

:!wc paper

where **wc** is the word count command, which counts the number of words (also lines and characters) in a file. This command will use the permanent copy of your file, not the temporary copy in the editor buffer. So normally when a command is given to the system while in the editor, a warning message is given if the file has been changed since it was last written. The autowrite option again allows you to give one command instead of two.

The final command for which the autowrite option works is the **Control–Z** command (see Sec. 8.2.4), which allows you to suspend your editing session and return to the system level. In almost all cases you will want to use the file you are editing, and obviously you will want an updated version to work with.

The autowrite option can be over–ridden in every case; **:next!, :rewind!, :tag!,** and **:stop!** will not write but will discard any changes in your editor buffer.

For some reason the command to edit a new file (**:vi**) does not autowrite, and you must give the sequence of commands

> **:w**
> **:vi newfile**

to write out the current buffer and edit a new one. On the other hand, with the autowrite option on, **:n newfile** will have the same effect. Since **:vi** will not edit multiple files (Sec. 7.6) and does not "work" with **autowrite**, **:n** should be used in all cases to start editing a new file from **vi**.

7.9.2 Writeany

The philosophy of the UNIX system is that the users know what they are doing and do not need elaborate schemes to protect them from destroying their files. Furthermore, the UNIX system has an excellent file backup mechanism so that the consequences of destroying files are rarely severe.

The Berkeley system certainly does not depart radically from that approach, but seems to want to hedge a bit. One result, as noted, is that the editor will not normally allow you to write into a file unless that file is either the file you are editing or a new (empty) file. Thus if you are working on a file called **paper1** you cannot write parts of it out to a file called **paper2** if the latter exists; this makes sense, since it would destroy the original contents of that file. However, most users would rarely do this. On the other hand I am constantly creating files called **junk**, which I use and then either rename or have no further use for. I often fail to remove them when through with them, and as a result get messages when I try to write part of my buffer to **junk**. Of course **:w! junk** will do the job; I prefer to use the **writeany** option which will allow me to write to any file I am allowed to write to.

Another Berkeley product, the C-Shell, has an option, **noclobber**, that has the same purpose as the write protections used by the editor. However, whereas the write protection (**nowriteany**) is the default with the editor, **clobber** is the default with the C-Shell.

7.10 ENCRYPTION

The **vi** editor has an option that allows you to encrypt text as it is being entered into your file, and to decrypt it for later editing. Furthermore, you can use the general system encrypting and decrypting program, **crypt,** to use that file with your programs. To edit a file with encryption you give the command (at the UNIX level):

> **vi –x** filename

You will then be asked for a key; it is not echoed to the terminal as you enter it. While this makes sense from a security point of view, if you make a mistake while entering it, you will lose your work. To read your file outside **vi,** give the command

> **crypt <** *filename*

You will again be prompted for the key, and if it is correct the decrypted version of your file will be printed on your terminal. If you are dealing with sensitive data, this is the best way to protect it, as nobody (not even the superuser or system administrator) can read it. Nor can they help you read it if you forget or mistype the key!

7.11 SUMMARY OF NEW COMMANDS AND OPTIONS

Only two new **vi** commands were introduced in this chapter. They are:

Control–]*	same as **:ta** with word after cursor as argument (7.7)
Control– `	same as **vi #** (7.5)

On the other hand, a large number of new **ex** commands, many being variations on the same theme, were introduced. They are:

:arg	list files being edited (7.6)
:f	show summary statistics of file (same as Control–G) (7.3.1)
:f *filename*	associate *filename* with contents of buffer (7.3.1)
:n	edit next file in argument list (7.6)
:n!	edit next file, discarding changes in current buffer (7.6)
:n *filelist*	edit *filelist* (7.6)
:r *filename*	read *filename* into buffer below current line (7.3.2)
:nr *filename*	read *filename* into buffer below line *n* (7.3.2)
:rew	rewind argument list (7.6)
:ta* *function*	move to defining line of *function* (7.7)
:ta!* *function*	move to defining line of *function* discarding changes in buffer (7.7)
:vi *filename*	read *filename* into buffer and edit it in visual mode (7.5)
:vi! *filename*	read *filename* into buffer and edit it in visual mode discarding changes in current buffer (7.5)
:vi#	read alternate file into buffer and edit in visual mode (7.5)
:w	write buffer to file it came from (7.3.1)
:w *filename*	write buffer to *filename* (7.3.1)
:n1,n2 w *filename*	write lines *n1* to *n1* of buffer to *filename* (7.3.1)
:w!	write buffer if system allows, overriding editor constraints (7.8)
:w >>*filename*	append contents of the buffer to the end of *filename* (7.3.1)

The following new options were introduced in this chapter:

:se autowrite	(aw, noaw) automatically write out buffer (if changed) before **:n**, **:rew**, **:stop**, **:ta**, or **:!** commands given in visual mode (7.9.1)

:se taglength = * *x*	(tl, tl = 0) only first *x* characters of tag are significant (7.7)
:se tags = * *path of files*	(tags, tags = tags /usr/lib/tags) path of files to be searched for tags (7.7)
:se writeany	(wa, nowa) allow user to write to any file the system allows him to (7.9.2)

Commands marked with an asterisk are not found in all versions of the editor.

NOTES TO CHAPTER 7

1. The mail system is a very useful system that beginners are usually not aware of; familiarize yourself with it soon.

2. Assuming that the system and the editor will allow you to write to that file. See Secs. 7.8 and 7.9 for a discussion of what files you can write to.

3. If you have not already done so, remove **common** with the command **rm common** before proceeding. Sec. 7.8 will explain why.

4. Rather, **was** on before it moved to the bottom line in response to the **:**.

5. At least on my DEC VT100 terminal. The **vi** documentation gives it as control-up-arrow, which does not work on my terminal. In any case, they clearly refer to the character with code 036 in octal notation. You should be able to find out how to send it from your terminal by consulting (or having a more knowledgeable colleague consult) the terminal's manual.

6. Not only are the named buffers saved, but so are the remembered search strings, last commands, and so on. Thus the **n** command entered immediately after a new file is edited will go to the last string you had searched for (in the previous file) and the **.** command will repeat the last change. Also, all options set during the current session are kept.

7. Note that the two **a**'s refer to two different things: the first one (preceded by a double quote) refers to the buffer in which you will yank the lines, and the second (preceded by a single reverse quote) refers to the mark you have used on the first line to be yanked.

8. With the **autowrite** option set (see Sec. 7.9.1) the current file will be automatically written out before a **:n** command.

9. Using UNIX metacharacters; thus **:n chap*** would edit all files with names starting with chap.

10. With the **autowrite** option on, the current file will be written out automatically.

11. Note that the **R** is upper case. The flag **–r** is used to recover lost files (Sec. 7.2).

12. Exactly the same effect can be obtained by giving the command **view decl**, which invokes **vi** in the read only mode. **View** is not available on all versions of the editor.

13. It is possible to over–ride this protection using the settable option **writeany,** discussed in Sec. 7.9.2.

8

Miscellaneous Commands

The commands described in this chapter are very important ones that did not fit into any of the previous chapters. They fall into three groups:

1. *Search and substitute commands.* We have briefly mentioned searching for a pattern in Chap. 4, and will discuss complicated search and substitute procedures in Part III. Here we will discuss those aspects that are likely to be used while in the screen mode.

2. *Commands to the UNIX operating system.* We have mentioned them briefly in Chap. 5 and 6; we will here give a more formal description of their uses.

3. *The abbreviation and macro capabilities of the editor.* These allow single keystrokes to reproduce sequences of instructions. They can be very useful if certain long sequences of keystrokes are often used, otherwise they may be just an amusing diversion from the task at hand.

8.1 SEARCH AND SUBSTITUTE COMMANDS

In the stand-alone use of **ex** these two commands are used together very often. In the screen or visual mode, the search command is used far more often than the substitute one.

8.1.1 Searching

The search command is the most useful way of moving long distances over text; it is also a useful way of moving over shorter distances. The normal way of using it is to enter a /, which will appear on the bottom line. Then enter the text being searched for, ending it with a **CR**. Note that this shows that searching is, in a real sense, an **ex** command, a point not stressed in Chap. 4. The cursor will either be placed on the next occurrence of that pattern, or, if the pattern does not occur, you will get the message: "Pattern not found" on the bottom line.

Searching is the only convenient way to move large distances through a big file. Let's assume that you are writing a paper and have processed a first draft using the document formatting program **nroff** or one of its derivatives. You have a dozen pages of printed output, and you want to make a few changes. You could start at the top of the file and scroll down, correcting the mistakes as you reach them. With a small file that has many mistakes it might be an appropriate method, but with a large file (and especially with a slow terminal) that has few mistakes, you would spend most of your time just watching the text scroll by! The best approach is to look for an uncommon word close to the place you want to reach and search for it. If it does not get you there[1], the **n** command, repeated once or twice, should. Remember that **n** will search for the last string or pattern given to it.

A second use is for moving over short distances. There are several ways to move to a word that is three or four lines away. One way, perhaps the most common, is to get there by moving to the start of the appropriate line (using the **CR** key to go down or the — key to go up) and then use the **w** key to get there. An alternative way is to get to the correct line and use the **f** command to get at or near the word. A third approach is to use the search command to get there in one step, or close to it if the word is very common. Even in the latter case, a single search command followed by two or three **n** commands is often the fastest way of getting there.

8.1.2 Patterns

Patterns, the things that are searched for and substituted, will be discussed in great detail in Part III. Here they will be discussed enough to allow you to use them effectively for searches from the visual mode.

By and large, patterns are made up of a string of characters, including blanks, that are to be exactly matched in the text. Thus the command

/ boy

will search for the next occurrence of the three letters making up that pattern, whether they occur as a complete word or as part of a longer word such as "boys."[2] On the other hand, it will not match "Boys," because of the upper case letter.[3] The entire pattern must be found on the same line in the text for a match to occur; thus the search command

/boys will be boys

will fail if the phrase is spread over two lines.

Up until now you have dealt with "normal" characters which have no special significance. There are certain characters, called **metacharacters**, which have a special significance. The caret (^) and dollar sign ($) signify the beginning and end of the current line (Sec. 4.3.2) respectively. Thus

/^boy

will not search for a caret (^) followed by the letters making up boy, but will search for boy at the beginning of a line. Similarly

/ boy$

will search for the word boy at the end of a line. These symbols are only meaningful at the start or the end of a pattern respectively and lose their significance in any other position. Thus

/ boy^

would search for that particular pattern of three letters followed by a caret, an unlikely pattern that is probably an error! On the other hand you may really want to search for something with a dollar sign, and

/$100

will search for that sum of money.

There are five other metacharacters that have special meanings in search patterns: they are **.**, *****, **[**, **]**, and ****. Their special meanings will be discussed briefly below, and in more detail in Chap. 10; for most screen editor searches these are just a nuisance. Since the characters (except for the period) are not very common, you may just try not to use them in search strings; if you have to you must precede them with a backslash, which makes them lose their special status.[4] Thus if you want to search for the string "$10.00" you would give the command

/$10\.00

If you find them turning up too often, you can set the option **nomagic**, which will turn off the effect of all metacharacters except for ^, $, and ****. In the unlikely event that, after having turned them off with the **nomagic** option you would want to use their properties, preceding them with a backslash will restore their potency.

There are two uses of metacharacters that are useful in screen mode. The first deals with matching patterns only if they are found at the start or end of words. The command

/ \<boy

will only match boy at the start of a word; thus it will not match "flamboyant," but will match the start of "boycott." On the other hand the command

  / boy\ >

will only match boy at the end of a word. It will not match "boycott," but will match "busboy." Can you guess how we can match boy, and only boy? It is easy:

  / \<boy\ >

will do it.

This is useful not only in searching for words in text, but also in looking for specific variables in programs. Remember the definition of an ordinary word (Sec. 4.3.1): a sequence of alphabetic or numeric characters or a sequence of special symbols. The first definition is close to that of a variable in most programming languages. Suppose you want to go through a program finding all uses of the variable "i." Searching for "i" alone would turn up an immense amount of irrelevant matches; all languages have an "if" statement, some kind of integer declaration, other keywords such as "include" and "define" (in C), or "begin," "while," "until" (Pascal), to say nothing of variables like "big," or comments like "...this function will...". Thus a search based on "i" will not be very fruitful. On the other hand, a search based on **/ \<i\ >** should turn up no extraneous matches.

A second moderately useful feature is the ability to include a class of characters in the pattern by including them in brackets. Thus **/[bB]oy** will find any pattern that includes either "boy" or "Boy." Character classes may be defined in two ways: by explicitly including them (as in the above example) or by giving a range. An example of the latter is **/i[3-6]**, which will match "i3," "i4," "i5," or "i6." It also is often useful in searching programs.

If this has whetted your appetite to know more about the use of metacharacters in searching, go on to Part III. If, on the other hand, you find the logic of this approach tortuous, forget all about it. Metacharacters are fun (for some of us), but not necessary for daily work in the visual mode.

A final option dealing with searching is the **wrapscan** option. It is normally on, and a search will, if need be, wrap around the end of the file. In the rare cases when one does not want this to happen, one can turn it off with the

:se nowrapscan

command.

8.1.3 Substituting

This is used far less often in screen editing than in line editing. Suppose you have this line in your file

Now is the time for all good man

and want to replace "man" with "men." The simple way to do so is to get to the word, position the cursor over the "a," and replace it by an "e." An alternative way is to position the cursor anywhere on that line and give the command

:s/man/menCR

Note that this is an **ex** command; hence the colon which appears on the bottom line and the **CR**. As you may have guessed, the command has three parts: the **:s** is the name of the command; the string between the slashes is the pattern to be replaced, and the final string is the replacement pattern. Look carefully as you press the **CR**; the cursor will flash to the place where the change is being made and then return to its original location.

Why would anyone go through such a complicated process? For a single substitution, the **vi** approach is clearly simpler than the **ex** one. However, the **ex** substitute command can do things that are less easily done in the visual mode. For example, when you want to make the same modification in several different places in a file, it will save you the need to search for each one and redraw the screen. This is called global substituting, and is an essential component of any usable editor.

Suppose that you have written a paper in which you used the abbreviation "USA," and you later decide that you would rather spell it out in full. How would you go about making the change? Obviously you could search for each occurrence of "USA," the first time with the command **/USA**, then with the simple **n**. When you find the first instance you would probably use

cwUnited State of AmericaESC

For each subsequent change you should use the **.** command, to repeat the last change command. If the paper is long, you will spend a lot of time watching the screen scroll by as you move from one instance of the abbreviation to the next. To see what happens when you make substitutions on many lines, enter the following little file:

This country is the USA. The Fourth of July is a holiday
in the USA. My terminal is made in the USA.
Her brother is in the USAF.

In the first example of the substitute command you did not give any line numbers. In such cases the command is executed on the current line (the one that the cursor is on). You may, however, have a command executed on a series of lines; in such cases you precede the command by the range of lines over which it is to act (first line, comma, last line).[5] The lines may be referred to by line numbers, by marks, or by context (the last alternative is discussed in Part III). In this case you want to make the change on all lines. You can easily see that there are three lines, so you could enter

:1,3s/USA/United States of America

In many cases, including this one, you want to make a change over the entire file, and while it is not difficult to find the number of the last line (**Control–G** will get it for you) it is simpler to refer to it simply as **$**, so you might use

:1,$ s/USA/United States of America

The expression **1,$** is so common in ex that it has been given a special symbol: **%**, so the final form of our instruction would be

:%s/USA/United States of America

Give any of these three instructions and see what happens. The first line is processed as you want it to be; the single occurrence of the abbreviation is expanded. On the second line only the first of the two substitutions takes place; the second abbreviation remains. Finally, on the third line, an inappropriate substitution takes place. The first problem is the easier of the two to deal with. The substitution command normally only changes the first occurrence of a pattern within a line; if you want all occurrences to be changed, append the letter **g** (for global) to the command. To show that the **g** is the global flag, not part of the replacement pattern, put a slash at the end of the replacement pattern and before the **g**:

:%s/USA/United States of America/g

Undo the effect of your first attempt to make the changes with a **u** command and give the second version of your substitute command. The substitution will occur on both instances of USA on line two; you will again have an inappropriate substitution on line three.

There are two ways to solve the problem of inappropriate substitutions. The first involves metacharacters; as you may have guessed

:%s/ \<USA\ >/United States of America/g

will do what you want. In this particular case it is probably the most appropriate solution.

The second solution has the advantage of being more general. It involves using a second flag with the substitute command **c** (for confirm). Undo the last substitution again, and give the following command:

:%s/USA/United States of America/gc

On the bottom line of the screen you will see the first line of your file with carets under the three letters "USA," followed by the blinking cursor. If you now enter **yCR** the substitution will be carried out; it you enter anything else (including just **CR**) it will not. Enter **yCR**; nothing visible will happen, but the substitution will be carried out. In any case, you will be presented with the next line, with the carets under the first "USA." Again enter **yCR**; you will now be presented with the line again. This time the first "USA" will have been expanded, and the carets will be under the second instance. Again request the change; you will now get the third line. Just entering **CR** now will request no substitution. Now that the entire file has been processed, you will get a request to enter **CR** to continue; the screen will be updated, and you will find all the appropriate substitutions carried out.

The advantage of using the confirm flag is that there will be times when you will not want to make the substitution everywhere the pattern occurs, even when suitably defined. Thus you may want to change Chapter to Chap. except when it is the first word of a sentence. Not even **ex** can determine whether a word is at the beginning of a sentence; you will have to see it and decide.

What advantage does global substitution have over the first method suggested, namely to search for **USA** and carry out a substituion using the **.** command for all except the first? In such a small file there is no advantage, but in a more realistic example you would have a lot of scrolling in the visual mode, as opposed to being presented with just one line at a time in the **ex**–based method.

Furthermore, there will be times when you will be confident that you do want to make all substitutions. For example, just after entering the previous sentence I invoked the spelling checker on the file containing the text of this chapter (you will see later how to do it) and found that my file contained one or more instances of the word "numgber" which is clearly a misspelled "number." I had no doubt that I wanted all instances of that pattern changed, so I unhesitatingly gave the command

  :%s/numgber/number/g

The moral is clear: if you are sure that you will want to make the change everywhere, use a simple substitution command; if in doubt, use the **c** flag. The main use of the unflagged command is for spelling mistakes, but even here you will probably be more comfortable using the **c** flag.

8.1.4 Global Commands

Very closely related to the search and substitute commands are the global commands, which will be described fully in Sec. 10.3. In their full generality they take the form

:*n1,n2g/pattern/command***CR**

All lines from *n1* to *n2* are searched for *pattern*. In the very common case in which you wish to search the whole file, no range is given. On those lines where *pattern* is found, *command* is executed. This is again one of the very important commands for systematic file modification. In the screen mode it is often used to print all lines containing a specific pattern. For example, if while editing this chapter I wanted to see all lines with the pattern **:s** (to see all the examples of substitute commands I have given) I would enter

:**g/:s/p**

where **p** is the **ex** print command. This will, of course, not show me lines with **:%s**; these can be found by a second separate search or by the use of metacharacters. Another such command that I often give while writing is:

:**g/ ^/ .sh/p**

This will print all lines which start (did you notice the caret?) with a period (it is a metacharacter, so it must be escaped) followed by the letters "sh." The macros I use for formatting use that combination to signal a section heading, so the command shows me the section headings in the current file.

Another common use of global commands is to delete lines with a specific pattern. A simple example would be to delete all comment lines in a FORTRAN program. I specifically chose FORTRAN because in that language comment lines must have the letter c in the first column. The following would do it:

:**g/ ^c/d**

where **d** is the delete command in **ex**.

8.2 COMMANDS TO THE OPERATING SYSTEM

The **ex** editor can use ordinary UNIX commands in a variety of ways. You may divide these interactions into four groups:

1. Commands which act only on the buffer's copy of the file being edited, and have no effect on any of the permanent files in the system.
2. Commands which only involve files in the system, and have no effect on the editor buffer.
3. Commands which may involve both.
4. A pair of commands that suspend the editing session and invoke the editor with the diagnostic output of language compilers.

8.2.1 Commands Acting on the Buffer

These commands take a range of lines in the buffer as input and replace them by the output of the command. The most used is the **fmt** command described earlier; it takes a set of ragged lines and replaces them with a smooth set. The range of lines is normally specified as being from the cursor to any **vi** object, thus

!*object command*

(with no space between *object* and *command*) is the prototypical command. If you have !! the object is a number of lines, specified before the command:

n!!*command*

will send *n* lines to *command*. If the object is not a set of lines, its description can be preceded by a count. For example,

!2{**fmt**

will format the next two paragraphs, while

!1G**fmt**

will format text from the start of the file to the current line. Note that the ! does not appear on the bottom line until you have fully specified the object on which it is to act. The cursor moves back to under the ! while the command is executing, a process that may take some time.

Such commands are often said to "filter" portions of the buffer. In UNIX terminology a filter is a command which takes an input stream, modifies it, and outputs it. Since a portion of the buffer is used both as input and output, such commands cannot have any effects outside the buffer.

An interesting situation occurs when you make a mistake in entering the name of the command to be executed on your text. The text is taken away to be given to that command and be replaced by the latter's output. Since a nonexistent command has no output, the net effect is that the text sent to the command is deleted. Once again, **u** comes to the rescue!

8.2.2 Commands Not Affecting the Buffer

These are commands to the UNIX system which have access to all your files but do not have access to your buffer. They act very much as if you were at the UNIX prompt level; the only difference is that after the command you are back in the editor. In fact, they act by creating (the word "spawning" is often used) a new instance of the shell program. On some systems you may in fact get a modified prompt when in such a secondary shell. To give the command you just enter

:!command

Note the colon, showing that this is an **ex** command unlike that described in the previous section. You will get the UNIX prompt on the bottom line, followed by the output of the command (after it has finished executing—you may have to wait for some time). Then you will get a second prompt, indicating that the command has been executed and that you are back in the editor. This will be followed by a line telling you to hit **CR** to redraw your screen and be in the editor again.

What kinds of commands does one use while in the editor? Basically you can divide them into commands related to the current editing session and unrelated commands. Most commands related to the current editing session are best given in the third format (see below).

The unrelated commands are legion. While editing you may wish to know if a specific user is logged on, to see if any mail has come,[6] to check your directory to find the exact name of a file that you are about to read into your buffer, or to send mail to an associate asking for information you will need to complete the paper you are currently working on. In all cases you could exit the editor, do the job, and return to editing, but it is simpler just to give a command and continue editing.

8.2.3 Commands Involving Buffer and Files

There are two flavors of commands that may involve both the buffer and the permanent files: those taking input from the buffer (and potentially writing output to permanent files) and those putting their output in the buffer, often taking their input from permanent files.

The first group are treated as a variant of the write command in that the contents of the buffer (or part of them) are written into a command. Their general format is

:*n1,n2***w** !*command*

In the very common situation in which you want the whole file to be the input to the command, just leave out the line numbers. If you want to know how many words your file currently contains, the following command will give you the answer:

:**w** !**wc** −**w**

You have certainly come across the **wc** command by now. It will count the number of lines, words, and characters in a file. If you do not specify any flags, it will print out all three counts. The −**l**, −**w**, and −**c** flags will cause it to print out only the information requested. Thus the command as given will only print out the number of words. If the file is for the document formatter, it will contain extraneous instructions which should not be included in the word count; these can be removed by a program called **deroff**. The following command combines the effects of **deroff** and of **wc:**

   :w !deroff | wc –w

Here the vertical bar stands for the UNIX **pipe** symbol. A pipe (Sec. 12.2.1) takes the output of one program and makes it the input of the next. Here **deroff** takes the contents of your buffer as input. Its output is the contents of your buffer minus any word processor commands and would normally be printed on your terminal. In this example its output is instead used as input to **wc,** which thus counts the number of words in your buffer after the extra symbols have been removed.

   The opposite command is clearly

   :n r *!command*

which will take the input of *command* and put it in your buffer after line *n* (the current line if *n* is omitted). Try giving the command

   :r !date

This is what I got into my buffer when I gave it:

   >% Mon May 30 18:03:58 EDT 1983[7]

Notice the prompt; it consists of two characters rather than the usual single one. I have arranged my account so that any sub–shells will give a distinctive prompt, reminding me that I am in a special shell. A more useful example would be to sort the contents of an unsorted file while reading them into the buffer.

   I regularly use the **:r** command in conjunction with the UNIX spelling checker. The command, at the UNIX level, of

   spell *filename*

will give an alphabetized list of the words in *filename* that the spelling checker believes to be wrong. The problem of finding the words in *filename* and correcting them remains. An alternative is to give the command from within **vi** and to read its output at the end of the file. First write out the file being edited with a **:w** command, then give the command:

   :$ r !spell %

The first part of the command, **:$ r**, asks that the output of the command should be read into the file after the last line, so as not to mess up the real text. The **%** symbol represents the name of the current file (Sec. 7.5), so the results of running the spelling checker on a current copy of the file (remember you just wrote it out) will be put at the end of your buffer.

    Now you can check each word on that list. If it is a correct word that the checker did not accept, delete it from the list. If it is indeed a misspelling, you can search for it in the file, correct it, and then delete it from the list.

8.2.4 Miscellaneous UNIX Commands

    The first of these is the **Control–Z*** command, only available with the full Berkeley C shell. It is a general command available to all programs when running the C shell, and it temporarily suspends their execution. They may be resumed, at the exact point at which they were suspended, by a command of **fg** (for foreground). I do not want to go into the details of the C shell, but will point out that it is very useful when you are repeatedly modifying and using a file, as you can go back to editing it without the overhead involved in starting up an editor session.

    A classic example occurs when using the programming languages lisp or prolog, both of which are interpretive. They

---

    *This command is not present in all versions of the editor. Throughout this book, all commands (whether editor or UNIX) that may be absent, or function differently, on certain systems will be marked with an asterisk. These differences will be discussed in App. E.

both use files produced by the editor, and the easiest way to make changes is to interrupt the editor after having made the file, then enter lisp (or prolog). When you want to make a change in your file, interrupt lisp with a **Control–Z** and resume the editor. After making your changes, interrupt the editor and resume lisp. In practice it is much easier than it sounds.

The UNIX command **error***, also a Berkeley product, takes the diagnostic output of the language compilers and puts it into the source file as comments. These comments start with the string **###** and end with **%%%**, and are hence easily searched for. Furthermore, if the **–v** flag is given to **error** it will invoke **vi** on each file containing errors, positioning the cursor at the first error.

The following very short C program, assumed to be in a file called **badhel.c**, has a parenthesis missing before the semicolon.

```
main()
{
    printf("Hello, world\n";
}
```

To compile it invoking **error** I used ordinary **cc** command and piped both standard and error output to **error** with the command (using the C shell):

cc badhel.c |& error –v

The expression **|&** pipes both outputs to **error**, and the **–v** flag invokes the editor. The editor was invoked, and the file now had the following appearance:

```
main()
{
/*###3 [cc] syntax error %%%*/
    printf("Hello, world\n";
}
```

It is a very useful tool, and if it is available on your system use it.

8.3 ABBREVIATIONS AND MACROS

Version three of the **vi** editor has some very powerful facilities for using abbreviations and macros. Both of these allow you to replace long sequences of keystrokes by shorter ones, and in many cases by single ones. The difference between abbreviations and macros is that abbreviations are effective in text insertion mode, while macros are effective in command mode. There is a flavor of macros that acts in text entry mode, which will be discussed with the abbreviations.

While both only act in **vi** mode, they are set in **ex** mode (just as are all options). Like options, they may also be stored in the **.exrc** file and be automatically set every time the editor is invoked. In a sense they both allow you to customize the editor.

8.3.1 Abbreviations

Abbreviations are set using the **:ab*** command in the **ex** mode. The full syntax of the command is:

:ab *lhs rhs*

Whenever *lhs* is entered *as a whole word* it is expanded into *rhs*. To give an example, if you want to use U as shorthand for UNIX, enter

:ab U UNIX

and whenever you enter U as a whole word it is changed into UNIX. Thus if you start a sentence with "Ultimately, we..." the leading U does not expand into UNIX. The definition of a word is almost that of our "small" words in that it is a collection of letters and numbers ended by a nonalphanumeric character. However, it must be preceded by a blank; thus, in this example U. or U" will be expanded, while "U will not.

Abbreviations can, after expansion, occupy more than one line, so their definition may contain **CR**s. But how do you enter a **CR** into the definition, given that defining an abbreviation is an **ex** command and that **CR**s terminate **ex** commands? The answer is to strip **CR**s of the ability to end a command by preceding them with a **Control–V**. Thus if I wanted to map nut into

> Department of Nutrition,
> Harvard

I would enter

> **:ab nut Department of Nutrition,Control–VCRHarvardCR**

On entering the first escaped **CR** it appears as **^M**, understandable when I realize that **CR** transmits the same computer code as does **Control–M**. The second **CR** terminates the abbreviated command.

While this command is most often used to abbreviate long expressions that are often used, it may also be used to correct common spelling errors. The two most frequent errors that the spelling checker turns up on my files are "similarily" and "foreward." I could eliminate them by giving the pair of commands

> **:ab similarily similarly**
> **:ab foreward forward**

While I have not done so, it is fun to know that I could if I wanted to.

The command **:ab** with no arguments will list the abbreviations currently active. Abbreviations can be removed from the list of abbreviations; the command to do that is called, rather appropriately, unabbreviate, abbreviated to **:una***. It does not work on abbreviations with embedded **CR**'s in them, as **vi** cannot handle multiple line text on the bottom line. To unabbreviate such abbreviations, temporarily enter **ex** mode with the **Q** command, unabbreviate in **ex** mode, and return to **vi** mode with the **:vi** command.

The second flavor of abbreviation is similar in syntax to macros, with which it is normally grouped. Since it acts in text entry mode, it is here grouped with abbreviations. Its syntax is very similar to that of the macros*:

> **:map!** *lhs rhs*

where *lhs* should normally be a single character (obviously a seldom used one; the control characters are the best candidates). It differs from the usual abbreviation commands in that as soon as it is entered at the keyboard, it gets expanded, whether it is a separate word (as is needed with abbreviations) or is immediately followed by other alphanumeric characters. These macros can be unmapped by the command*:

:unmap! *lhs*

while **:map!** with no arguments gives you a list of currently mapped macros.

8.3.2 Macros

While abbreviations replace patterns during text entry, macros do the same at the command level. The syntax of the commonest variety is similar to that of abbreviations*:

:map *lhs rhs*

where it is, to all intents and purposes, essential that *lhs* be a single character, while *rhs* is a sequence of control level commands. The main (or only) difficulty with this approach is that almost every key already has a function assigned to it. There are, however, a few keys with no functions. They are

Control keys:	Control–A, –K, –O, –T, –V, –W, –X
Upper case:	K, V
Lower case:	g, q, v
Symbols:	*, \, — (underscore)

Any of these may be used as the *lhs* of a map command. Macros may be unmapped with the **unmap*** command

:unmap *lhs*

and the list of currently mapped macros may be displayed by the command **:map** with no arguments.

Let me begin with an example of a repetitive series of commands I often give. When inserting a new sentence between two existing ones, I do not like to use the insert command, but prefer to split the line in two at the end of the first sentence and add the new material between the lines using the **O** command. How do you split a line containing two sentences?

Edit the **decl** file and move down to the line in the second paragraph that reads

of Happiness. That to secure these rights,

First you must move the cursor to the start of the second sentence; **a)** command will get it on the "T" of "That." An **h** command will get it onto the preceding blank, while an **X** will remove the blank before the cursor, leaving it unmoved on what was the second[8] blank. Now replace that blank with a **CR** using the **rCR** command and you are done.

While executing this command sequence is not a lot of work, it would be nice if you could store it and execute it with a single keystroke (or perhaps two). The simplest process is to define one of the keys of the keyboard to invoke this sequence. The following command makes the **g** key act as a "line splitting" command:

:map g)hXrControl–VCRCR

Why the Control–V and the two **CR**s? The Control–V gets the first **CR** into the macro definition, and the second **CR** ends the **ex** command.[9]

I constantly use a macro to check the spelling of a file, using the approach described in Sec. 8.2.3. Its implementation as a macro is

:map v :wControl–VCR:$r !spellControl–VCRCR

The two **Control–VCR** combinations enter two **CR**s into the definition, while the final **CR** ends the **map** command.

A variation on the above theme uses the function keys found on many terminals. The command*:

:map #n *rhs*

will map function key *n* into the *rhs*. In terminals with no special function keys you can still use this, entering the two key sequence **#n** instead of the function key.

The other way of storing macros uses the named buffers to store the sequence of instructions, which is then invoked by preceding the buffer's name by the @ key. To enter the line splitting sequence into buffer **z** you would first enter it as text on a line of its own, using an **o** command. Then you would delete it into that buffer with a **"zdd**. Now giving the command **@z** will split the line. There is no way of finding what macros are stored in the buffers or of specifically deleting them, though there is no problem in replacing their contents (just delete or yank new stuff into them).

8.4 SUMMARY OF NEW COMMANDS AND OPTIONS

In this final chapter on visual editing you met your last three **vi** commands. Those marked with an asterisk are not found in all versions of the editor.

Control-Z*	suspend currently active UNIX command (8.2.4)
!*object command*	send lines from current line to *object* to *command,* and replace them by its output (8.2.1)
Q	enter **ex** mode from **vi** (8.3.1)

In contrast, as you approach the **ex** section, the number of **ex** commands increases:

:!*command*	spawn new shell to execute *command,* return to editor (8.2.2)
:ab* *lhs rhs*	whenever *lhs* occurs in input as a word, replace it by *rhs*
:*n1,n2***g/***pat***/***command***CR**	find lines between *n1* and *n2* which contain *pat,* then do *command* on each (8.1.4)
:map*	list currently active macros (8.3.2)

:map* *lhs rhs*	replace *lhs* by *rhs* in command mode (8.3.2)
:map!*	list macros currently defined (8.3.1)
:map!* *lhs rhs*	whenever *lhs* occurs in input, replace by *rhs* (8.3.1)
:*n***r** *!command*	execute *command* and place input in buffer after line *n* (8.2.3)
:s/*pat***/***repl*	replace first occurrence of *pat* by *repl* on current line (8.1.3)
:una* *lhs*	*remove lhs* from list of abbreviations (8.3.1)
:unmap* *lhs*	remove *lhs* from list of macros (8.3.2)
:unmap!* *lhs*	remove *lhs* from list of macros (8.3.1)
:*n1,n2***w!** *command*	send lines *n1* to *n2* of buffer to *command* (8.2.3)

Finally, a few options related to the commands introduced in this chapter:

:se ignorecase	(ic,noic) ignore distinction between upper and lower case in searches (8.1.2)
:se magic	(magic, magic) metacharacters have their normal significance (8.1.2)
:se wrapscan	(ws, ws) searches will wrap around past end of file (8.1.2)

NOTES TO CHAPTER 8

1. The reason for not getting where you want could be a misspelled pattern, otherwise it would be that a similar pattern occurred earlier in the file. To minimize this occurrence, try to search for an uncommon pattern.

2. Or boycott or flamboyant, to say nothing of boysenberries!

3. In fact, not necessarily so. There is an option, **ignorecase**, which as its name implies leads to ignoring the case in making matches. It is a useful option if you are scanning the text for all references to a word.

4. The term **escape** is often found in the UNIX literature to describe this process. The concept of characters which have a special value, which can often be escaped with a backslash, pervades UNIX.

5. The resemblance to the syntax of the full fledged write command is not accidental. All **ex** commands share the same fundamental syntax.

6. Most new users take a long time to realize how useful (and fun) the UNIX mail facility can be. Find out more about it soon!

7. This records for posterity the way I spent the Memorial Day weekend of 1983!

8. Remember that the definition of the end of a sentence is a period followed by a newline or two more blanks.

9. Note that the documentation makes very heavy weather of entering control characters into macro definitions from **vi**. It appears that when it was written, **vi** always operated with the **beautify** option on. With **nobeautify**, currently the default, things are much simpler.

A CUSTOMIZABLE EDITOR

One of the many attractions of the **vi/ex** editor is that it can be customized to each user's specifications. There are three ways in which it may be customized: to use a variety of terminals, to select options, and through the abbreviation and macro capabilities, to redefine commands (within limits).

As noted at the start of Chap. 6, the editor needs to know what terminal you are using. Computers running **vi** have a file, **/etc/termcap**, that contains descriptions of many of the more common terminals. If you use a terminal not described in that file, someone will have to write a new entry in it, describing the terminal. The coding of the characteristics of a terminal is tedious, and the description in the UNIX documentation (under **termcap** in Sec. 5 of the manual) is terse. A longer description is given in a series of three articles by Bill Tuthill in the first three issues of UNIX/WORLD (see App. F for details). Note that the information in that file is available to any person that wants to use it.

Different users will have different tastes about features, as well as genuinely different requirements. Thus it can be useful to think of the settable options as being divided into "taste" options and "need" options. The former include such things as window size, autowrite, and writeany options. The latter include things such as autoindent, which is needed for programming but undesirable when entering text, and wrapmargin, which is needed for text entry but undesirable for programming. A user will probably always want the same set of "taste" options, but the "need" options may vary according to what he or she is doing.

Macros and abbreviations also may be divided into the same two categories. A user may well want to map certain keys, especially if he has function keys on his terminal, into common commands such as **dw**. This would be useful for either programming or text entry. On the other hand, the abbreviations used for programming are likely to have nothing in common with those used for text entry.

How can a user have a different set of options depending on what he is doing? You noted in Chap. 6 that the editor begins by looking for a file called **.exrc** in the user's home directory, and if it finds it reads and executes the commands in it. Since there is only one such file it would seem to be impossible to have more than one set of options read in. Fortunately there is a command, **:so** *filename*, that will read the contents of *filename* and execute them.

As a general rule I keep programs and text in different directories, so the options I need depend on the directory I am currently using. I use this fact by having a **.exrc** file that contains my "taste" options, followed by the command **:so .set**. After these options have been set, the editor will look for a file called **.set** in the current directory and read and execute it if it finds it. I have such a file in all directories in which I do serious editing, customized to the needs of the type of work I do in that directory.

While I have described customizing the editor through **.exrc**, it is not the most efficient way of doing things. A slightly more efficient way is to set an environmental variable called **EXINIT** to contain the settings and abbreviations you want. That saves having to read the file **.exrc** every time you invoke the editor. How you do this depends, once again, on which shell you are using. Using the Bourne shell you would put in your **.profile** file

    EXINIT = 'set aw wa | so .set'
    export EXINIT

if you wanted to set the auto-write and writeany options in all cases. With the csh you would put

    setenv EXINIT 'set aw wa | so .set'

into your **.login** file.

MOVING UP TO EX

In this part you will study the line oriented component of the editor **ex**, and see what it can do for you. While it is much less suitable than **vi** for general editing, it is uniquely suited to the systematic modification of structured files. To understand this you must learn a bit about the context in which it was developed.

The **ex** editor is the direct desendent of the old UNIX editor, **ed**. That program was developed in the world of slow and noisy printing terminals. The flow of paper is always in one direction, and what has been printed on paper cannot be erased; thus it is clear that nothing like **vi** is possible. As a result **ed** used the entire line as its primary unit. One result was the extensive use of the **substitute** command, as noted in Chap. 8.

Let's amplify this point. Of the fundamental tasks of an editor, **ed** could easily be used to add whole lines, which is the fundamental text entry operation. It could just as easily delete whole lines. To add or delete parts of lines, however, the **substitute** command had to be used. In Chap. 8 you used **substitute** to replace one word by another; it is an easy extension to use it to add or remove text. Consider the following example. If in entering the Declaration of Independence you entered

Life and the pursuit of

you could correct it with the instruction

:s/Life/Life, Liberty

(try it out!). If, in a facetious mood, you had entered

Life, Liberty and the (alas! rarely successful) pursuit

you would have to give the unpleasantly long command

:s/ (alas! rarely successful)/

where the fact that there is no replacement pattern means that you want to replace the matched pattern by nothing (i.e., remove it).[1] Notice that the pattern to be removed has a structure. It consists of a space,[2] followed by a left parenthesis, followed by a whole lot of characters, followed by a right parenthesis. The notation of metacharacters, considered a nuisance in Chap. 8, now comes to your help. The command can be expressed in that notation as

:s/ (.*)

where the space and parenthesis represent themselves, the period represents any character, and the * stands for "repeated any number (including zero!) of times."

Necessity forced the users of **ed** to treat it almost as a programming language, useable for ordinary text entry; in addition, it is very useful for doing complicated text rearrangements. An example, to be studied in detail in Chap. 11, should impress you with the capabilities of **ex** (or **ed**).

Figure A shows a bibliographic citation retrieved from the National Library of Medicine's (NLM) MEDLARS bibliographic retrieval system. Its format is slightly different from that used by the UNIX reference retrieval system **refer**, shown in Fig. B. The differences are not great, but the effort needed to change a file containing a few dozen (to say nothing of a few hundred) citations from the one format to the other, line by line, is certainly far from trivial. Given the similarity between the two formats, it should be a programmable task.

```
8
AU – Barrocas A
AU – Webb GL
AU – Webb WR
AU – St. Romain CM
TI  – Nutritional considerations in the critically ill.
SO  – South Med J 1982 Jul;75(7):848-51
```

Figure A: Bibliographic item in NLM format.

Can you see how you would start to modify a file containing a large number of such entries? Note that the author entries in the NLM format all begin with **AU –**, while the corresponding UNIX lines begin with **%A**. It should be clear, then, that you can use the global command briefly described in Chap. 8 to change the one into the other. The command

> :*g/*^AU/s/AU –/%A

will first select all lines beginning with **AU**, then carry out the indicated substitution on them. You may guess how to make some of the other changes. Some, however, are more tricky: how do you put periods after the initials of the authors?

```
%Z 8
%A Barrocas A.
%A Webb G. L.
%A Webb W. R.
%A St. Romain C. M.
%T Nutritional considerations in the critically ill.
%J South Med J
%D 1982
%V 75(7)
%P 848–51
```

Figure B: Same item in UNIX format.

If that kind of thing interests you, read Part III. If it does not, you already know all you need to perform most ordinary editing tasks.

Chapter 9 covers all the **ex** commands that you have not yet met, introducing them in the context of using the editor to enter and modify ordinary text. While this may not be what you plan to use it for, you have to learn how to walk before you can run. Chapter 10 discusses the "magic ingredients" of **ex** and explains how they can be combined to form a powerful editing tool. In Chap. 11 you will use these commands to modify structured files and end by applying them to the problem just described. Finally, Chap. 12 gives a brief overview of several other UNIX tools that are useful for editing.

Many readers will never want to use **ex**; others will be using it much less than **vi**. Therefore it cannot be covered in as much detail as the **vi** editor. Appendix F refers to several good sources of information.

NOTES TO PART III

1. In this case, the second slash is redundant and can be omitted.

2. There is one space between the end of "the" and the left parenthesis, and a second one between the right parenthesis and the start of "pursuit." If you only removed the parentheses and the material between you would be left with two spaces.

9

EX COMMANDS

You now start your exploration of the **ex** editor as a tool in its own right, rather than as a set of commands invokable from the visual mode. To invoke **ex** you enter (at the UNIX level) the command **ex** rather than **vi**. The screen does not clear, nor does any part of your file get displayed. Instead, you will get, on the last line of the screen, a message followed by the **ex** prompt, **:**.[1]

Like the **vi** editor, **ex** has command and text entry modes (the latter often called the **append** mode, as the commonest way of entering it is to give the **append** command). It differs in that text can only be entered as whole lines (as with the **o** and **O** commands in **vi**), and commands take lines as their argument. A further basic difference is that in **vi** the screen shows you, at all times, the appearance of the part of the text that you are currently editing. The **ex** editor only shows you the last line it has done something to, unless you specifically ask it to show more of the file.

9.1 TRYING OUT EX

Now repeat your first exercise, entering a short file with many mistakes and making corrections, using **ex** instead of **vi**. Figure 9.1 gives a record of an editing session (note that it is much easier to record the behavior of a line oriented editor than of a screen one).[2] Try it out; reading is fun, but you must do things yourself to master them.

```
 1      % ex junk
 2      "junk" [New file]
 3      :a
 4      Now iss the for
 5      most good man to
 6      come come to the ad
 7      of their parti.
 8      .
 9      :s/i/y
10      of theyr parti.
11      :u
12      of their parti.
13      :s/ti/ty
14      of their party.
15      :-
16      come come to the ad
17      :s/come /
18      come to the ad
19      :s/ad/aid
20      come to the aid
21      :-s/most/all
22      all good man to
23      :s/ma/me
24      all good men to
25      :-s/s
26      Now is the for
27      :s/ f/ time f
28      Now is the time for
29      :1,$ p
30      Now is the time for
31      all good men to
32      come to the aid
33      of their party.
```

```
34    :x
35    "junk" [New file] 4 lines, 68 characters
36    %
```

Fig. 9–1: Sample **ex** session.

The first command to the UNIX system invokes the editor, which responds that **junk** is a new file and then gives the prompt. Since the file is new and thus empty, the only thing you can usefully do is put text into it. The **a** (for append) command will add text after the current line, in this case after the (non–existing) zeroth line. Once you are in append mode, the editor stops giving you the prompt, and you enter your text. Exiting append mode is done by entering a line with nothing on it but a period in the first position (line eight).[3] You immediately get the prompt in response;[4] the editor is ready to accept commands, and the last line entered is now the current line.

First try to correct the misspelling of the word "party" on the last line. The obvious way would be

s/parti/party

but entering five letters twice when only one needs to be changed does seem to be more work than is needed. What would happen if you entered

s/i/y

instead? Try it; you will find that it is the first "i" on that line (in the word "their") that gets replaced. As in **vi**, **u** comes to your rescue. On a short line such as this it is easy to see that

s/ti/ty

will do the trick, as there is no earlier occurrence of the pair of letters "ti."

A command of – will get you to the previous line and print it (line 16). The first of the two repetitions of "come," with the space following it, can be removed by the command

s/come /

where the second slash is redundant, and is merely given to show that there is a blank after the word. Try it out both with and without the slash to convince yourself that it works. Unfortunately, there is no command like the **dw** command in **vi** to remove a word and the following blank. The result of carrying out the substitution is printed out, and a second substitution corrects the remaining error on that line (lines 18-20).

All **ex** commands must refer to a specific line, which is normally the current line unless you instruct it otherwise. So far you have been satisfied with using the current line; in line 21 you will try something more adventurous. There are many ways of referring to lines, and Sec. 7.4 mentioned line numbers and marks. In this case it is clear that the next change will be on line two; this will usually be far less clear in a large file. You therefore often use relative line addressing; the – means the previous line. The remaining corrections are then made (lines 23-28) and on line 29 ask the editor to print out the whole buffer to be sure that no errors remain (and that no new ones have been introduced).[5] You then end the session with an **x** (for **exit**, or rather **xit**) command, which acts exactly as **ZZ** does in **vi**.

Before studying individual commands in any more detail, you should understand the structure of **ex** commands, and also the general principles on which line addressing is based.

9.2 STRUCTURE OF EX COMMANDS

All **ex** commands have a common structure. All need a range of lines (often implicitly specified) to act on. In addition, many require one or more parameters and accept optional flags. Less commonly they may have a variant form or take a count. Finally, they all may have comments and, with few exceptions, be stacked several to a line.

9.2.1 Addresses

Commands act on specific lines of the buffer and thus need to be told which lines to act on. As a general rule, if no line is given, the command will act on the current line. Addresses (as line numbers are often referred to) precede the command.

9.2.2 Variants

Some commands have a variant form differing in some detail from the standard, and obtained by adding a **!** immediately after the command name. You have met several, such as **:vi!**, in Chap. 7. Others will be described below.

9.2.3 Parameters

The command is often followed by parameters, such as the file to be read or written to, the substitution to be carried out, and so on.

9.2.4 Counts

Some commands may be followed by an optional count; thus **d5** will delete five lines, starting from the current one. On the other hand, **5d** will delete line number five.

9.2.5 Flags

There are three printing commands in **ex** (Sec. 9.4.3), abbreviated to **p**, **l**, and **#**. Following a command by any of these three abbreviations will cause the current line to be printed in the appropriate format. Since the default[6] for almost all commands is to print the current line after execution in the normal **p** form, it is rarely necessary to append **p** after a command. The **p** or **l** must be separated by a space, except in the case of **dp**. Any number of **+** or **−** characters (but not a count) may follow the flag; the corresponding offset will be added to the current line before printing it.

9.2.6 Comments

The double quote on an editor command line causes the rest of the line to be treated as a comment; it is rarely useful in normal editing but can be very useful in preparing editor scripts (Chap. 11).

9.2.7 Multiple Commands

It is possible (but rarely advisable) to put several commands on the same line, separating them by the | character. Comments, commands to the UNIX operating system, and global commands must be the last commands on a line.

9.3 ADDRESSING MODES

As noted several times, all commands need an explicit or implicit set of lines to act on. You will now see the fundamental ways in which lines can be addressed and how they may be combined. While few specific examples will be given, I strongly urge you to edit the **decl** file (give the command **ex decl**) and try out each type of line addressing mode described. Giving a single line address will cause that line to be printed, while giving a pair of addresses will cause the printing of all lines between them (inclusive).

Lines may be referred to in the following ways:

.	This is the abbreviation for the current line, almost always referred to as "dot." This is usually the last line affected by the previous command and is almost universally the default. Therefore there is little occasion to use dot alone as an address. On the other hand, dot is very often used as one end of a range of addresses, as in $\pm n$,., or .,/**pat**.
n	The nth line in the buffer, numbered sequentially from 1. It is a superficially appealing way of addressing lines, especially since the **nu** or **#** commands will print out the number of the current line, or a range of lines. The problem is that the addition or removal of a single line will change the numbers of all subsequent lines. I never use this mode and suggest that you do the same.
$	The last line of the buffer. This and the follow-

	ing are obvious exceptions to my rule against using specific line numbers.
%	An abbreviation for **1,$**, very useful for referring to the entire contents of the buffer.
±n	An offset relative to the current line. If the offset is 1 you do not need to enter it explicitly as in our example (lines 21 and 25). It is often used in the form

$$-n, +n\mathbf{p}$$

	to print some context around the current line (the **z** command is probably better).
/pat/?pat?	The first line, scanning forward or backward as the case may be, containing *pat*. If a command will follow the scan, the second **/** or **?** is needed, otherwise you can omit it as for **vi** scans. If the pattern is omitted, the last pattern specified is used.
	This is a bit more tricky than appears at first sight. You may get to a line with a pattern and perform a substitution on (or near) that line with another pattern. If you now give a **//** command, the pattern searched for would be the one used by the substitute command. To use explicitly the last pattern used in a scan you must use \/ or \?.
'''x	These have the same meaning as in **vi:** " refers to the last position of the current line before a non-relative motion, while *'x* refers to a line marked *x* with the **m** command.

    If you have been adventurous, you may have tried logical combinations of addressing modes. A simple example would be **$−5**, which should print out

    long established should not be changed for light

For a more complex example, get to the top of the file (**1** will get you there) and give the command

    /Life/−1,/Life/+1

You should get

> by their creator with certain unalienable rights,
> that among these are Life, Liberty and the pursuit
> of Happiness. That to secure these rights,

Do you see how the command in this example could be abbreviated? The second **Life** is redundant; giving a pair of slashes will make it search for the previous pattern, which is also **Life**. Furthermore, offsets of 1 do not need to be explicitly given; thus the command

/Life/ − ,// +

would have the same effect.

You have used the most common way of referring to ranges of lines: a pair of addresses separated by a comma. In this case the actual addresses of both target lines are computed from the current position of the current line. Can you see how this would lead to a problem in certain cases? Suppose that you want to print the line containing "Life" and the four lines that follow it. Would a command of

/Life/,+4p

given from line one do the job? Try it. You will get a message saying "First address exceeds second." Why? The computation of the line addresses took place while line one was the current line; hence +4 refers to line five, while "Life" is found on line 13. Since the request to print (or do something to) the line with "Life" on it and the next four lines is inherently reasonable, there is a way to do it. Using a semicolon in place of a comma as the address separator will cause the first address to be calculated relative to the current line. Dot is then reset to that address, and the address of the second line computed relative to the new dot. Try

/Life/;+4p

and you will get the desired result.

In using **ex** for general purpose editing, all of these addressing modes are used according to the current need. For modifying structured files, the most important is the pattern-matching mode, occasionally used with offsets.

9.4 ex COMMANDS

Having learned the structure of commands and addressing modes, you will now go over the whole set of **ex** commands by function. New commands are listed in alphabetical order at the end of this chapter, while all **ex** commands are listed in App. B.

9.4.1 Adding, Changing, and Removing Lines

In addition to **append**, there are two other text entry commands. To add text above the current line use **i** (for **insert**). To change one or more lines use **c** (for **change**) which will delete one or more lines and put you in text entry mode. All three are exited by typing a line with a solitary dot on it. At the end of a command which has added text, dot will be set at the last line entered. If you give a **change** command and add no text (i.e., immediately exit append mode with a dot) the current line is set as after a **delete** command.

These three commands will use the current setting of the **autoindent** option; the variants (**a!**, **i!**, and **c!**) will use the opposite setting, i.e., they will autoindent if it is off, and not autoindent if it is on. It is useful if you are entering text for which **autoindent** is usually set off and are entering something which you want indented.

Entire lines are deleted with the **d** command; you can delete either a single line (the current line is the default) or a range of lines.[7] After a delete command, dot is set at the line following the last line deleted. If the last deleted line is the last line of the file, dot is set at the new last line.

Just as with **vi**, material deleted is stored in the numbered buffers and can be recovered with the **put** command. Furthermore, with the delete command material can be saved in named buffers; thus

−5,.d a

will delete the current line and the five previous ones (for a total of six lines) and store them in buffer **a**. Note that you do not need to precede the buffer's name with a double quote.

9.4.2 Moving Lines

There are two commands which will move lines. The first command, **move**, abbreviated to **m**, will take a range of lines and put them after the destination given on the command; thus

*n1,n2***m***n3*

will put the lines from *n1* to *n2* after *n3*. What if you want to move them to before line one? You simply move them to after line zero.

Copy, abbreviated **co** so as not to conflict with **c**[8] (**change**), is identical to **move** except that it leaves the original lines in place. After both commands, dot is left at the last line moved.

This mechanism is a bit clumsy as you must refer, in a single command, to three lines. It is probably simpler to do as in **vi**,— delete the lines to be moved[9] and **put** them in their new location.

The **yank** and **put** (abbreviated to **y** and **pu**[10] respectively) commands of **ex** do what a **vi** user might expect. The **yank** command will yank a range of lines (or a count starting from a given line) into a named buffer, or the numbered buffer if no name was specified, and leave dot where it is. The **put** command will put the lines (from a named buffer, or the numbered one if no name is given) after the line specified in the command (dot is obviously the default), leaving dot at the last line put.

9.4.3 Printing Lines

There are three commands which print lines on the terminal. The most common is the ordinary **print** command, abbreviated **p**, which will print the range of lines specified in the command (default is dot). There are two variants. The first, **number** (abbreviated **nu**[ll] or **#**) will precede each line by its number. Furthermore, once it has been used, the printing that occurs automatically after most commands will be in numbered format till a **p** command is given. There is a settable option, **number**, which will cause this format to be used by default. Also when using this option, input lines will be prompted for by their numbers. Both are very useful if you want to use line numbers.

While not a printing command, **.=** will print the current line number. Note that it requires the dot to print the current line number; **=** alone will print the number of the last line, i.e., the number of lines in the file.

The second variant is **list**, abbreviated **l**, which was very useful with **ed** as that program did not list control characters in a visible way. With **ex**, which like **vi** shows all control characters except the tab and the end of line, it is of less use. It shows tabs as **^I** (tabs are represented internally as **Control–I**) and the end of line as **$**. Its only use is to find out at once if blanks in a line are tabs or spaces, and to see if there are any spaces at the end of a line. Like **nu**, once used it becomes the default mode until turned off with an explicit **p** command and is settable by a **list** option.

After all three print commands, dot is left at the last line printed, and all three can take a count of lines to print rather than a range.

There are a pair of other commands which can be used to show context, both similar to **vi** ones. The first is **Control–D**, which will scroll down exactly as it does in **vi**. The second is **z**, which takes a variety of forms. In its simplest form it takes a count (default window) and prints that number of lines starting from the addressed line (default dot plus one, as dot is presumably on the screen). In other words, it prints a window of text with the addressed line at the top. If the count is preceded by a **.**, the same amount of text is printed but with the addressed line in the middle, providing more context. If it is preceded by **−**, the addressed line is placed at the bottom of the window.

Both **Control–D** and **z** will print according to the setting of the **list** and **number** options.

9.4.4 File-Oriented Commands

Almost all the file oriented commands described in Chap. **7** were **ex** commands invoked from **vi**. They are, of course, identical when invoked from **ex** (except that there is no need for the colon). To edit a second file in **ex**, use the **ex** *filename* and its variants instead of **vi** commands. The command **vi** used from **ex** will get you into **vi** mode, with the cursor on what was dot in **ex**.

While in **ex** you cannot directly edit a second file in **vi** mode; that is, the command **vi** *filename* will not work, nor will **ex − v** *filename* (see App. D). You must do that in two stages, and there are two ways of doing it. You can either get into **vi** mode and give the **vi** *filename* command, or you can give an **ex** *filename* command and then change to visual mode.

You have noted above (Sec. 9.1) that the normal way to leave **ex** is through the **x** command. This will write out the file if any changes have been made and then quit. A very similar command is **wq**; the difference is that this will always write out the file, even if no changes have been made. It can take a filename as argument; in this case it will write the buffer into that file before quitting. Should that file exist, the command **wq!** will override any qualms the editor may have in writing to it (Sec. 7.8).

9.4.5 Commands to the Operating System

Most of these are identical to those described in the corresponding section of Chap. 8. The command

   n1,n2**! command**

will act like the **vi** command

   object!command

and filter the contents of lines *n1* to *n2* through *command,* replacing them by the output of command. Note the difference between the apparently similar commands *!command* and *n1,n2! command.* The former sends a command to the shell unrelated to the buffer (Sec. 8.2.2) while the latter is a command acting on the buffer (Sec. 8.2.1).

The **shell** command is similar to the **!** command except that while the latter only acts for a single shell command, the former spawns a new shell that is in effect till you explicitly leave it by entering a **Control–D** or **exit**. At that time you return to your editing session.

Finally, the **stop** command, only available on systems using the C shell, will suspend the editor command the way **Control–Z** does in the **vi** mode. If the autowrite option is set, it will write out the file before stopping. The variant command **stop!** will not auto-write, and may be used if that option is set and you want to discard changes made to the file.

9.4.6 Miscellaneous Commands

There is a **j** command very similar to the **J** command in **vi** to join lines. Normally it will join the next line to the current one, adjusting spaces as does the **vi** version. If it is given a range of lines, it will join them all into one line. The variant, **j!**, will simply join the second line at the end of the first, with no processing of white space.

The command **preserve** (no abbreviation) will preserve your buffer as if the system had crashed. It is used when you cannot write out your file (e.g., if the disk you use is full).

A related command is **recover** *filename*. It is an alternative to recovering that file with the **−r** option of **ex** (Sec. 7.2).

The command **so** (for **source**) allows you to read a file of editor commands, which will be executed as they are read. That is what happens to your **.exrc** file; you can **so** as many other files as you want. Such commands can be nested, i.e., a **sourced** file can **source** another one.

The command **version** (abbr: **ve**) will display the current version of **ex** and the date of its release.

9.5 SUMMARY OF NEW COMMANDS AND OPTIONS

The following new **ex** commands were introduced in this chapter:

Control–D   scroll down one window (9.4.3)
append   (abbr: **a**) append text after address (9.4.1)

change	(abbr: **c**) delete text addressed and replace by following (9.4.1)
copy	(abbr: **co** or **t**) copy addressed lines to after third address (9.4.2)
delete	(abbr: **d**) delete addressed text (9.4.1)
insert	(abbr: **i**) insert text before address (9.4.1)
join	(abbr: **j**) join lines smartly (9.4.6)
list	(abbr: **l**) print lines more unambiguously on terminal (9.4.3)
move	(abbr: **m**) move addressed lines to after third address (9.4.2)
number	(abbr: **nu** or **#**) print lines on terminal (9.4.3)
preserve	save buffer as if system had crashed (9.4.6)
print	(abbr: **p**) print lines on terminal (9.4.3)
put	(abbr: **pu**) copy lines from buffer into file (9.4.2)
recover	recover file from save area (9.4.6)
shell	spawn a new shell (9.4.6)
source	(abbr: **so**) read a file and execute instructions in it (9.4.6)
stop	suspend editor command (9.4.6)
version	(abbr: **ve**) display version number of editor (9.4.6)
yank	(abbr: **y**) copy addressed lines into buffer (9.4.2)
z	print a window of text in the appropriate format (9.4.3)
=	print number of addressed line ($ default) (9.4.3)

The following new options were introduced in this chapter:

autoprint	(ap, ap) print result after most commands (9.2.5)
list	(list, nolist) print lines more unambiguously (9.4.3)
number	(nu, nonu) automatically number lines (9.4.3)
prompt	(prompt, prompt) set prompt in **ex** (9)
terse	(terse, noterse) suppress long error messages (9.2.5)

NOTES TO CHAPTER 9

1. One of the things **ed** was most often criticized for was the lack of any prompt. For diehard **ed** users who think that they do not need one, there is a settable option, **prompt**, which can be set to **noprompt**. Treat this as interesting information for a trivia quiz, and do not even consider turning the prompt off!

2. The line numbers shown in Fig. 9–1 were added for your convenience; they are not produced during the editing session.

3. Note the similarity to the text insertion mode in **vi**, where you need an **ESC** to get out. In **ex**, however, no number of **ESC**'s will get you out of append mode; they will be quietly entered into your file.

4. Thus you can always tell if you are in command or append mode; in the former you get the prompt after each command has been executed (essentially after each **CR**), while in the latter you get no prompt.

5. Note that in **vi** you would not need to print out the file; it is there on the screen.

6. In deference to **ed** users, there is a settable option, **autoprint**, which can be turned off to suppress normal printing. There is also an option, **terse**, which can shorten the error messages that **ex** gives. I would strongly advise against using either.

7. Alternately, for both the **c** and **d** commands, you may specify a starting address (default dot) and a count of the number of lines to delete or change. Thus **d5** and **.,+4d** both delete five lines starting from dot.

8. Since **ed** only supported single letter abbreviations, **copy** had to be called **t**, which stood for **transpose** or **transport**.

9. Or **yank** those to be copied.

10. So as not to conflict with **p** for **print**.

11. Note that **n** represents **next** (Sec. 7.6).

10

THE MAGIC
INGREDIENTS

There are three elements of **ex**, all borrowed from **ed**, that give it its great power to edit structured documents. Most were initially thought of as aids to entering text with **ed**, but it was soon realized that they changed this editor into a kind of programming language. The three magic ingredients are:

1. Pattern matching.
2. Substitution.
3. Global commands.

The first two were present in some form in almost all the then existing text editors. What distinguished **ed** from other editors was the care with which these other elements were implemented, and how well they worked together. Let's discuss them in turn. If you have not read Sec. 8.1, do so carefully before going on. This chapter is a continuation of the material discussed there, which will not be repeated.

10.1 PATTERNS

In Chap. 8 you saw many of the building blocks out of which patterns are made. The most fundamental is a series of ordinary characters which will be matched by that same series appearing in the text. You noted that obtaining a match might not produce the one you wanted, and that the shorter the series of characters (refer to it from now on as a string) the more likely an inappropriate match. Thus, if in **decl** you were at the top of the file and wanted to get to the word "indeed" in the final paragraph, you might try to get there by giving the command **/ind**, guessing that there would be no other words containing that collection of letters. You would, however, find that "mankind" does end with those three letters. If you return to the top of the file and try **/inde**, you will get where you want.

More complex expressions can be made up by using characters which have been given a special significance; they are called "metacharacters." You have met some of them in Chap. 8. Two of them deal with the position of the string in the line; $^\wedge$ will match the string at the beginning of the line, and **$** will only match it at the end.[1]

You have also met the metacharacters that match at the beginning or end of words, **\<** and **\>**. They can obviously be combined; thus **/\<end\>** will match the complete word "end" wherever it occurs as a complete word (but will not match "ending"), while **/^\<end\>** will match it only if it occurs at the start of a line. How do you match it occurring alone on a line? This should be easy: **/^ end$**. Since it is the only thing on the line, there is no need to specify that it must occur as a word. What does **/ $** match? A line with a blank as its last character, almost certainly an unintended result. And what about **/^$**? A line with nothing on it.

10.1.1 Character Classes

The next type of metacharacter is the character class. At its simplest it is a set of characters between brackets; any member of that set will match. You saw in Chapter 8 that **[bB]oy** will match "boy" or "Boy." What would **h[ie][mr]** match? It would match "him" or "her" (as well as "hir" and "hem," and any other word including these strings).

The contents of a character class do not have to be letters; thus **[,;:.!?]**[2] would represent the most common punctuation marks.

A more interesting situation arises when you include a much larger set of characters in the class. If you wanted to match any upper case character you could use **[ABC...XYZ]**, entering all 26 letters. There obviously has to be a better way! Indeed there is, and you can abbreviate the above to **[A–Z]**. Now what does **/^[A–Z]** match? Any line starting with an upper case letter. What about **/^[A–Z][a–z][a–z][a–z] /**? A line starting with an upper case letter followed by three lower case ones, followed by a blank; which adds up to a line starting with a capitalized four letter word!

Character classes specified using the range method should be carefully thought out, as the range refers to the order of the characters in the internal code of the machine. On almost any computer the following three are safe: **[A–Z]**, **[a–z]**, and **[0–9]**, together with any subranges of the above. Do not try things like **[A–z]** (upper case A to lower case z) unless you know exactly what you are doing![3] What if you want – or] to be part of a character class? For – you have a simple solution, since if it is the first member of the class it cannot be a range indicator. Escaping by preceding with a backslash will work in either case. How do you get a backslash into a character class? By entering it twice in succession.

A variant that is often useful is the negation of a character class. Thus **[^abc]** means any character other than a, b, or c. More useful would be **[^a–z]**, which represents everything except the lower case letters.

Character classes come into their own when used in conjunction with other metacharacters. I nevertheless want to give a realistic example of their use before going further. What do you think

/(19[0–9][0–9])

matches? It matches 19 followed by any two digits, the whole number between parentheses, which is almost certain to be a publication date if the document being scanned follows some of the popular systems for citations.

The next metacharacter is the dot, which has so many uses in the editor. As part of a search string it represents any character; thus **x.y** will match x+y, x/y, or xty (as in sixty). It can be useful alone, for example to find expressions involving x and y, but one often runs into problems. Thus **x.y** will not match x + y, since there are three characters (space, plus, space) between the x and the y rather than one. Its main use is in conjunction with the star metacharacter.

10.1.2 Closures

The asterisk or star, *, means the character (or character class) which preceded it repeated zero or more times. The technical name for this is a closure. You have already seen an example in the Prologue to this part, where it was explained that **(.*)** means a left parenthesis, followed by an arbitrary number of characters, followed by a right parenthesis. Thus, if you have

   y = a*(b + c)

and you want to change it to

   y = a*x + z

you would give the command

   s/(.*)/x + z

For an example dealing with English text, suppose you have

   This is a very extremely messed up and bad sentence.

and you want to change it into

   This is an improved sentence.

One way, of course, would be to delete the whole line and re–enter it, i.e., change it. Another way would be to give the command

s/a very extremely messed up and bad/an improved

This may well take longer than changing the whole line, especially if you make an error and have to redo the substitution. Do you see how the combination of dot and star can help you? Try

s/ a .*bad/ an improved

and see if it gives you the required change. Note the redundancy in your substitution command. The initial "a" is the first on the line; give a space before and after it to be sure. Suppose that the string had ended with a "d" instead of spelling out "bad." Would the search have ended at the first "d," at the end of "messed"? Try it out; you will find that it has the same effect. The search is for the first suitable match, extending as far into the line as possible.

Now let's look for some more structured patterns. What does

/[a–z][a–z0–9]*

match? It matches something that begins with a lower case letter, followed by zero or more lower case letters or digits. In many programming languages, that represents an identifier. Let us add a bit to it:

/[a–z][a–z0–9]* *(

This represents an identifier, followed by zero or more spaces, followed by a left parenthesis, and, in a language which does not use parentheses for arrays (such as C or Pascal), it will represent a function or procedure definition or call.

Star can also be combined with negated character classes. Suppose you have a name file which contains the last name, comma, space, first name or names or initials, one entry being

Jones, Jack C.

How can you best refer to the last name? One way would be

[A–Z][a–z]*

which is simple but longer than needed. You used the fact that a last name is an upper case letter followed by zero or more lower case ones, which is perfectly true. But you made no use of the fact that, in this file, last names are ended by a comma. Thus you could have used the shorter expression

[^,]*

which means a string of non–commas. Such a string is ended as soon as you reach the first comma.

It was mentioned that the pattern matched will be the one that starts first and is as long as possible. This can lead to unexpected results in long lines of text, especially if you are not careful. Let's return to your example involving parentheses, and suppose that you have

text (a silly comment) more stuff (a good comment)

and want to delete the silly comment. Do you see what **s/ (.*)** would do? It would delete all the line after the blank preceding the first parenthesis. How can you remove the first comment only? You must produce a pattern which will not match the whole line; a safe way would be **s/ (.*) m /m**.

A second point that causes a lot of problems is that star means zero or more occurrences of the character being matched. The classic mishap is if you have

abcdeeeeefg

and want to change the multiple "e's" to a single one. The obvious way is to give the command **s/e*/e**, which you hope will change the many "e's" into a single one. Alas, it does not. Try it out. How did it manage to add an "e" at the start of the line? It found zero or more (in this case, zero) "e's" before the "a" and replaced all zero of them by a single "e," inserting it at the start of the line! To make sure that you do not match zero "e's" you should give the command *s/ee*/e*, which will search for an "e" followed by zero or more additional "e's," i.e., for one or more.

There is a last type of metacharacter which divides the string matched into separate parts. Since the use of this is even more closely tied to substitutions than the rest of this section, it will be discussed with them.

10.2 SUBSTITUTIONS

You have seen the fundamental substitution command in Chap. 8. It is essentially

s/*pat*/*repl*

where you replace *pat* by *repl*. If *pat* is not given, the last search pattern is used. On the other hand, if no *repl* is given, *pat* will be replaced by nothing, i.e., will be deleted. However, the command **s** alone, i.e., with both arguments omitted, will simply repeat the last substitution command. A synonym for it is **&**.

In this form **s** acts on the current line, and the line is printed out after the substitution is made. It is very common to want to make a substitution on a range of lines; in this case it will only print out the last line on which the substitution is made. Furthermore, dot will be set to that line. To print out each line after the substitution has been made, you have to use a global command and explicitly give the **p** flag after the **s** command. Thus

%s/*pat*/*repl*/**g**

will change all occurrences of *pat* to *repl*, printing out the last change only, while

g/*pat*/**s**//*repl*/**gp**

will print out all lines on which the substitution takes place.

Note that normally you do not need a slash after **repl**. If anything is to follow it, such as a flag, comment, or continuation, the second slash is needed to separate it from what follows. In that case the line will not be printed after the substitution unless an express **p** flag is given.

Any of the metacharacters discussed above may be contained in *pat*. In many cases *repl* is simple text, especially when **ex** is being used to enter ordinary text. The general approach in that case is to try and match the material to be removed with as few keystrokes as possible, and then enter the replacement in full.

The characters which have a special significance as part of *pat* lose that significance in *repl*. Thus while **s/./,** will replace the first character of the line by a comma (probably not what you intended),[4] **s/./,** will work, since dot is not a metacharacter in the replacement pattern.

Before going on to more complex things, a note on how to split lines with **ex**. You cannot just give **CR** as the replacement, as a **CR** will end the substitute command. How then do you split a line between two words? As usual, the way to make **CR** lose its property of being the character that terminates commands is to precede it with a backslash, so

    s/*word1 word2*/*word1*/ \CR*word2*CR**

will do it. The first **CR** is treated as a character in the replacement pattern, while the second one will end the command.

The simplest replacement metacharacter is ~, which denotes the last previous replacement pattern. Thus if you have just given the command

    s/boy/child

and you come across the word "girl" and wish to change that also into "child," you can simply give the command

    s/girl/~

Of course, if you had come across a second "boy" you could have changed it with a simple **&** command.

The next replacement metacharacter is **&**,[5] which stands for the text that has been matched. Thus if you have

    Now is the time

the command **s/the/the best** can be shortened to **s/the/& best**. It can be combined with metacharacters in the search pattern, and can be repeated in the replacement pattern. What will you get if you give the command

s/.*/&? &!!

on a line containing "Now is the time"? Try it out and try to understand it.

The entire line will be matched by **.***, since this represents anything repeated any number of times, and the editor looks for the longest possible match. Therefore **&** will stand for that entire phrase. The replacement pattern is therefore the phrase, followed by the query, two spaces, the phrase a second time, and finally two exclamation marks. The result is thus[6]

Now is the time? Now is the time!!

How do you enter a true **&** in a replacement pattern? Do you really need to ask by now?[7]

So far you have used the **&** merely as a shorthand, to save a few keystrokes in situations in which you could have written out the replacement in full. Let's return to the example of the bibliographic file discussed in the Prologue to this part.

The last line in the example was

SO – South Med J 1982 Jul;75(7):848–51

The SO stands for the source of the citation. It is followed by the name of the journal, the year of publication, the month, volume, number in parentheses, and inclusive pages. How could you put the year in parentheses?[8] If you had a single citation there would be no problem; **s/1982/(1982)** would do it. You could of course save yourself a few keystrokes by using the ampersand: **s/1982/(&)**. But this is not necessary. Now if you have a large file containing similar citations, you will want to replace each year, whatever it may be, by itself in parentheses. The command would be (go back to Sec. 8.1.4 if you have forgotten about global commands):

g/^SO/s/19[0–9][0–9]/(&)

if you assume that all citations are from 1900 or later.

In a sense, using **&** assigns the pattern matched to a variable that you can use in building up the replacement pattern. If you could extend this idea to splitting the matched text into several variables, you could then rearrange them in the replacement pattern.

Let's go back to your file of names:

    Doe, Jane
    Jones, Jack C.
    Smith, J. H.

and suppose that you want to invert the names, giving you

    Jane Doe
    Jack C. Jones
    J. H. Smith

If the file is as short as this it may well be faster to re–enter the names in the proper order, but for one that is even slightly longer it can become unpleasant.

In this case you should put the last name in a variable, say *var1*, skip the comma followed by one or more blanks, and put the rest of the line into a second variable, say *var2*. You would then replace your pattern by *var2*, followed by a blank, followed by *var1*. To put part of a line into a variable that is later referred to, it is preceded by \(and followed by \). The first such variable is referred to in the replacement pattern as **\1**, and so on until **\9**.

Let's apply this to our example. The resultant substitution pattern is unreadable if given immediately in full, so let us build it up together. We noted above that the last name could be referred to as [^,]*, and in fact we gave that example in preparation for this. Hence to put the first piece of the substitution pattern in *var1* we use

    \([^,]*\)

which is not easy reading but should be understandable. The second piece, which we will discard and hence do not need to allocate to a variable, is simply

, *

and the final piece is simply everything that remains on the line, allocated to the second variable:

\(.*\)

The replacement pattern will simply be

\2 \1

so the substitution command, in all its glory, will be

s/ \([^,]*\), *\(.*\)/ \2 \1

It is, in fact, easier to enter such a command slowly at the terminal, thinking about each piece separately as you are entering it, than to read and understand it.

Now try to think how you would edit that file if, in addition to the names, it had telephone numbers at the end of each line.

Doe, Jane	2-1234
Jones, Jack C.	2-2345
Smith, J. H.	2-6543

It is clear that our former approach to identifying the first name and/or initials will no longer work. Why? How easy or difficult it will be to transpose the names depends on how the numbers are separated from the names. If they are separated by a tab it is very easy; the second variable becomes simply [^ **tab**]*, where you would enter a tab rather than spell it out.

If they are separated by a varying number of spaces it becomes rather tricky. The first variable and the following piece (comma and spaces) are unchanged. The second variable consists of zero or more characters from a class consisting of letters of both cases, blanks, and periods. Can you therefore refer to it as

[A–Za–z .]*

Try it out; you will see that it does not do what you want. The problem, of course, is that this definition includes the blanks that separate the first name or initials from the number. You need a pattern of zero or more characters as defined above, with the added proviso that the pattern should end with a lower case letter (if you have a name like Jane) or a period (if you have an initial). Hence the second variable escalates to

[A–Za–z .]*[a–z.]

If the file is at all long you may (and probably should) worry that in some cases the final initial may not be followed by a period; in this case the second pattern should also include the upper case letters. The resulting substitution, with that precaution added, takes the very complex looking form

s/ \([^,]*\), *\([A–Za–z .]*[A–Za–z.]\)/ \2 \1

Do you see why the first pattern is so much simpler than the second? The first is followed by a comma, and there can be no commas inside it, while the second is followed by blanks, and since they can occur inside it they do not serve as delimiters. Using a tab to end the field would therefore have made your task of modifying the file much easier.

Tabs are a very convenient way of separating fields, as they are unlikely to occur within those fields, as opposed to spaces. Indeed, the common assumption of many UNIX programs is that tabs will be used to separate the fields. I encourage you to use them whenever possible.

10.3 GLOBAL COMMANDS

These are the last of the three magic ingredients, often used in combination with the other two. As noted in Sec. 8.1.4, the general format of a global command is

n1,n2g/pattern/command

It was mentioned in Sec. 8.1.4 that these commands at their simplest can print out lines containing a given pattern. They can also be used to do more complex things. Returning to your bibliographic example, if you want to put the year of publication in parentheses you could give the command

g/^SO/s/19[0–9][0–9]/(&)

This would affect the 19[0–9][0–9] expressions only on lines beginning with SO.

The global command acts in two stages. In the first it marks the lines in the file that meet the condition, and in the second it executes the command (or commands, as you shall shortly see) on each marked line. This is very important; consider what would happen to the following if the command searched for lines matching the pattern and executed the commands as it went along:

g/*pat*/co$

This command finds lines which match *pat* and copies them at the end of the file, where you will perhaps use them to construct an index. If the command went along the file finding such lines and copying them as it went, it would loop infinitely. Fortunately, nothing the command does can change which lines will be affected.

A variant form of **g** which will select all lines that do not match a pattern is sometimes useful. It is referred to as **v** (for variant, the **ed** term) or **g!** (using the **ex** terminology for variant commands).

As a simple example of what you can do with global commands, enter a small file containing the numbers from one to nine, each on a line. To invert their order, each number (line) in turn is moved to the top of the file, i.e., moved after line zero. The easiest way to refer to each line is to give the pattern ^, since each line has a start. The following command will do it:

g/ ^/m0

Global commands act on matching lines in the entire file unless a range of lines is specified. What would happen if, in the previous example, you had given the command

2,$g/^/co0

Think first, then try it out.

You can enter multiple commands after a global (obviously excluding further globals, as that would confuse the marking of the lines). With **ex** you can enter them on one line, separated by |'s. An alternate way is to put each on a separate line, by preceding each **CR** (except the last which terminates the global command) with a backslash. Thus if you wanted to replace the initial few characters by %J on all lines starting with SO in the bibliographic example, and simultaneously put the year in parentheses, you could give the commands

g/^SO/s/SO –/%J/\CR
s/19[0–9][0–9]/(&)CR

The first substitute command now needs a slash after the replacement pattern to separate it from the escaped **CR** which precedes the second substitution. Alternately, you could have put both substitute commands on the same line, separating them with a |:

g/^SO/s/SO –/%J/ | s/19[0–9][0–9]/(&)CR

While this is a matter of personal taste, I do not like multiple commands per line, especially when they are at all complicated.

A common use for global commands is to delete lines which match a specified pattern.[9] Less well known is the use of global commands to enter text. You can give an **a**, **i**, or **c** command as part of a global; all you have to do is escape each **CR** with a backslash. If the text entry is the last part of the global command there is no need for a final line with a solitary dot on it; however, it does no harm and I normally put it in whether it is needed or not.

Let's now add once more to the bibliographic example. In the NLM format there are no blank lines between items, while the UNIX format requires a blank line at the end of the set of lines representing each citation.

g/^SO/s/SO –/%J/ \CR
s/19[0-9][0-9]/(&) / \CR
a \CR
\CR
.CR

Again, the **CR** at the end of each line except the last one is escaped. You have now had to add a final slash after the end of the substitution pattern on the second line.

A final note: global commands can use all addressing modes, and can act on multiple lines. Thus

g/*pat*/–2, + 2p

will find each instance of *pat* and print a five line window around it.

NOTES TO CHAPTER 10

1. This is a slight oversimplification: see the complete discussion in Sec. 8.1.2).

2. Note that the dot looses it special significance inside a character class.

3. This would match all upper and lower case letters as well as six special characters that have nothing in common except that their internal representation in most computers places them between the upper and lower case alphabets.

4. To replace the first period on a line by a comma, you should enter **s/\./,;** the backslash changes the dot from a metacharacter to an ordinary one.

5. Not to be confused with the use of **&** as a command to repeat the previous substitute command.

6. This very nice example is from "Advanced Editing on UNIX," by Brian W. Kernighan (see App. F for full citation).

7. In case you want to be sure, precede it with a backslash.

8. Putting the year in parentheses is not part of the transformation to UNIX format that will be described in the next chapter. It is, however, an interesting exercise in its own right and you will use it again later in this chapter.

9. In Sec. 8.1.4 you saw how that could be used to remove FORTRAN comments.

11

COMPLEX CHANGES AND EDITOR SCRIPTS

In Chap. 10 you learned the basic tools needed to make complex changes in structured files. You will now practice using them on a series of problems of increasing complexity.

A certain knowledge of the UNIX system is needed for a full appreciation of this material. I will, however, try to explain each concept briefly as it comes up. Let's start with input output redirection, a fundamental concept.

11.1 INPUT OUTPUT REDIRECTION

The output of most UNIX programs appears on the terminal, and the terminal as an output device is usually referred to as **standard output**. It is possible, however, to make the output go instead (redirect it) to any file with a simple change to the command line. If *program* normally sends its output to the terminal, the command

program > filename

will cause its output to go into *filename*, creating the file if it does not exist and destroying its old contents if it does.

For a simple example, the command **who** lists the users currently on the system, and its output appears on the terminal. Try the command

who > junk

You will see no output on your terminal, just the UNIX prompt coming back to you after a short interval. The output has been placed in **junk** rather than on the screen, and the command

cat junk

will show you that it is indeed in that file.

If output that normally appears on your terminal is called **standard output**, what can input that you normally enter from your terminal be called? Clearly it is called **standard input**; if there is any symmetry, it can be redirected, coming from a file. In fact, input is redirected in almost exactly the same way as output, and the command line

program **<** *filename*

will make *program* read its input from *filename* rather than from **standard input**. Now **ex** is a program whose input comes normally from your terminal, and so it should be possible to put a set of commands into a file and have them executed. Note that this is usually not desirable, as normal editing is a highly interactive process. If you are often going to give the same complex set of editor commands, for example to transform a file of bibliographic citations from one format to another, you will find it much easier to put the commands in a file and edit noninteractively.

Let's begin, however, with a trivial example. Figure 11–1 shows part of the contents of the file **junk** that I obtained as above.

```
ellozy     tty13 Jul 28 11:59
sixao      tty14 Jul 28 13:22
toray      tty16 Jul 28 13:35
linda      tty25 Jul 28 13:21
```

Fig. 11–1: Sample output of **who**.

Suppose that I want to keep only the names, sorted alphabetically. To strip off everything but the names would require the **ex** command

   %s/ .*

The pattern matches one blank followed by anything; thus everything from the first blank onwards is discarded. What remains is the name. Sorting the names is easy

   %!sort

will send the whole file to **sort** and put the output of sort where the unsorted names were. A final command of **x** will save the modified file. Try using **ex** and giving these commands to be sure that it works properly (quit using **q!** to keep the original form of **junk**).

   Now make a small file containing the three commands needed to modify **junk**, calling it **makename** or whatever else you want (Fig. 11–2).

   %s/ .*
   %!sort
   x

Fig. 11–2: File of **ex** commands.

Now try giving the command

   ex junk < makename

The effect will be the same as if you had edited **junk** and given these commands yourself. In fact, the messages you would have received had you been editing the file appear on the terminal (we will see later how to stop them). Files of commands to the editor are called **editor scripts**.

11.2 SHELL PROCEDURES

The next step up is to create files containing sequences of instructions to the UNIX system, rather than merely to the editor. If you want to find out who is on the system and would like to have an alphabetized list without any of the extra information **who** gives, you would have to give the **who** command and redirect its output, then give the **ex** command with input redirection, then **cat** the resultant file. Surely there is a way of automating this procedure?

The UNIX system command interpreter (the program that interprets what you enter at the terminal) is called the **shell**, and from now on you will use that name rather than the rather non–specific term "the UNIX system." It is possible to write a file containing a set of commands to the shell and have the shell read the file and interpret the commands as if you had entered them at the terminal. Such files are called **shell scripts**. Let's now make such a file to find out who is on the system. Figure 11–3 shows one way of doing it.

```
who > junk
ex junk < makename
cat junk
rm junk
```

Fig. 11–3: Command file to print names of users.

Enter the commands in a file called **dowho** or something similar and give the command **dowho**. The shell will give you a message "**dowho** not executable" or something similar. Ordinary files are considered not to contain comands, and thus are not executable.[1] Making a file executable is no problem; the command

```
chmod +x dowho
```

will do it. The **chmod** command changes the mode of the file, and **+x** tells it to add **x** (for executable) to the file's attributes. Now give the command **dowho** again. You should first get the editor's side of the "dialogue," followed by a list of the names of the current users. Shutting up **ex** is simple; edit **dowho** and replace **ex** by **ex–**. The minus is a flag that abolishes the editor's responses and is specifically intended for non–interactive editing.

11.2.1 A Practical Example

You now understand enough to be able to look at an interesting example. This book was written on the UNIX system, in a separate directory called **book**, which contained the text entered as well as a whole lot of small programs to help with the writing and modification. Each chapter went in a file named **chap***n*, and each appendix went in one named **app***n*. Initially I had referred to the control key as **CTRL**, which is the way it is labeled on my terminal. I ultimately decided that I preferred **Control**. I could, of course, have edited each file successively and given a command of

> **%s/CTRL/Control/g**

As there were 16 or 17 files at that time, the idea was not too appealing. To automate the procedure I first wrote a little file called change consisting of two lines:

> **%s/CTRL/Control/g**
> **x**

The second step was to get a file containing the names of the files to be modified. There are several variants of the command **ls**, which lists the files in your directory. One of them, **ls–l** (the final **l** stands for long format) guarantees that there will be one file per line on the listing. Thus the command

> **ls –l app* chap* > mybook**

put in the file **mybook** a list of the files with names beginning with **app** or **chap**. Figure 11–4 shows part of the resultant file. Notice that the filename follows the last blank of the line. Editing **mybook** and giving the two commands

> **%s/. * / ex – /**
> **%s/ $ / < change**

replaced everything before the filename by **ex–**, and added **<** **change** after the filename. The first substitution looked for the longest string of characters ending with a space. This ended just before the filename, so all that material was removed and replaced with the **ex–** command. The second substitution is obvious (there is no need for the spaces which surround the **<**, but I find that they increase legibility). Figure 11–5 shows the result. All that remains is to exit, change the mode, and give a command of **mybook**. It took some time to run; there were over 250,000 characters in the combined files at that time!

```
–rw–r––r–– 1 ellozy        6614 Jul 24 06:37 appl
–rw–r––r–– 1 ellozy        4671 Jul 14 07:28 app2
–rw–r––r–– 1 ellozy         886 Jul 14 07:17 app3
–rw–r––r–– 1 ellozy        8988 Jul 20 07:22 app4
–rw–r––r–– 1 ellozy        5077 Jul  6 18:11 chap0
```

Fig. 11–4: Start of **mybook** file.

```
ex – appl < change
ex – app2 < change
ex – app3 < change
ex – app4 < change
ex – app5 < change
ex – chap0 < change
```

Fig. 11–5: Start of **mybook** file after modification.

11.3 A MAJOR EXAMPLE

Having seen how to make small changes in structured files, let's return to the bibliographic example. Figures 11–6 and 11–7 show a citation in NLM and UNIX formats respectively (from the Prologue to Part III).[2] In addition to the differences shown, the lines relating to a single item must be followed by a blank line in the UNIX version. The question is: how do you transform a large file from the former format into the latter?

```
8
AU – Barrocas A
AU – Webb GL
AU – Webb WRA
AU – St. Romain CMAB
TI  – Nutritional considerations in the critically ill
SO  – South Med J 1982 Jul;75(7):848-51
```

Fig. 11–6: Bibliographic item in NLM format.

```
%Z   8
%A   Barrocas A.
%A   Webb G. L.
%A   Webb W. R. A.
%A   St. Romain C. M. A. B.
%T   Nutritional considerations in the critically ill.
%J   South Med J
%D   1982
%V   75(7)
%P   848-51
```

Fig. 11–7: Same item in UNIX format.

Some of the changes are almost immediately obvious. Changing the characters which identify the type of line, and adding the needed blank line at the end involves the commands given in Fig. 11–8. Note the slashes at the end of the replacement patterns on lines one to four. They are only needed on line four, but since you may end up modifying some of the other lines, it is safer to put the final slashes in.

```
1    g/ ^[0-9] /s/^/%Z /
2    g/^AU/s/AU –/%A/
3    g/^TI/s/TI –/%T/
4    g/^SO/s/SO –/%J/ \
5    a\
6    \
7    .
```

Fig. 11–8: First Commands for File Transformation.

The commands on lines one to four change the identifier from one format to the other, and are totally straightforward. While on the line starting with SO, you add the blank line that delimits the set of lines for a single item with the three commands on lines five to seven. Since lines four to seven are a single global command, the **CR**'s at the ends of lines four to six must be escaped.

That leaves you with only two problems: how to deal with the remaining initials (number unknown) and how to split the source line. The latter is the simpler problem. You can attack it from either direction. If you are willing to assume that there can be no colon on the source line other than that preceding the page numbers, you could give a command like

```
s/:/ \
%P/
```

This will replace the colon by an escaped **CR**, with the new line following starting with the %P, followed by a blank. A similar approach would be to chop off the volume number from after the semicolon. The question is: can you be absolutely sure that the journal title will contain no colons or semicolons? That is a dangerous assumption, especially as a safer alternative exists.

The year of publication is clearly a very stable landmark ending the title, as few medical journals have a date number as part of their title.[3] The last global command created a blank line following the source line, and left dot there. You can modify line seven by escaping its **CR**, calling the modified line 7'. You could continue as follows, noting that you want to change the line before the current dot:

```
7'        .\
8        –s/ *19[0-9][0-9]/ \
9        %D &/
```

You have now split the original line into two fragments:

```
%J South Med J
%D 1982 Jul;75(7) :848-51
```

The next break in that line is obvious; you want to replace the space, month, and semicolon by a **CR** followed (at the start of the newly created line) by %V space. The simple way to do this is

```
g/^%D/s/ [A-Z].../ \
%V/
```

The problem with this approach is that it assumes that the file is **exactly** as it ought to be. When dealing with a structured file you must assume that it has more or less the structure you expect, but defensive programming requires you to make as few assumptions as possible. A safer approach would therefore be

    10 g/^%D/s/ *[A-Za-z][^0-9]*/ \
    11 %V /

This time you are looking for one or more spaces followed by one or more nondigits. This allows for more spaces than expected, for a month starting with a lower case letter, and for a greater or smaller number of characters than expected before the volume number is finally reached. However you choose to do it, you should end up with the following:

    %D 1982
    %V 75(7) :848-51

Breaking up this final piece is trivial:

    12 g/^%V/s/:/ \
    13 %P /

I have left the problem of putting a period followed by a space after each initial for the end. You do not know how many initials there are. The simplest approach is probably based on the realization that the last initial is an upper case letter followed by the end of line, while all others are upper case letters followed immediately by another upper case letter. The following should get you close:

    2' g/^AU/s/AU −/%A/ \
    2a s/ \([A-Z]\)\([A-Z]\)/ \1. \2. /g

This is one of those initially frightening commands that are not really difficult to understand if studied one piece at a time. Look for two adjacent upper case letters, put each one in a separate "variable," and replace that pattern by each letter followed by a period and a space. Then add the global suffix to carry out this substitution on all pairs of successive upper case letters.

You still have some work to do. If there are an even number of initials, all would seem to be in order, but the period following the final initial is followed by an unwanted space. If there are an odd number of initials, the last will be unmatched, and so will not participate in the substitution. Thus you escape the **CR** at the end of line 2a, add lines 2b and 2c

> **2b s/ $// **
> **2c s/[A-Z]$/&.**

and you are through.

Or are you? This will work only if there are no errors in the file and no pairs of consecutive upper case letters found in the name. If you can avoid that assumption, you will be that much safer. Unfortunately, safer approaches can only put in one period at a time, so you must guess what is the largest number of initials you will ever need to modify.

You can start putting the periods in from either end of the string of initials. Start from the end, first putting a period after the last initial. This is easy; **s/$/.** will do it. You now want to put a period after the previous initial. It is an upper case letter followed by an upper case letter and a period, so the following should do it:

> **s/ \([A-Z]\)\([A-Z]\.\)/ \1. \2/**

The following shows what happens after you give that command the first time:

> %A St. Romain CMA. B.

Each time you repeat this command (all you need is a single **&**, as I hope you remember) one more initial will have a period and space appended. The final form of the commands to modify the author line is thus

> **2' g/^AU/s/AU −/%A/ **
> **2a'   s/$/./ **
> **2b'   s/ \([A-Z]\)\([A-Z]\.\)/ \1. \2/ **
> **2c'   & | & | &**

What happens if you give the command after all the initials have been modified? Nothing, as no match will be found. You must therefore guess what the maximum number of initials you can expect to find is (say five) and put in an appropriate number of repetitions of the command. Thus if you expect a maximum of five initials, process the first one with line 2a; line 2b will process the second one, while line 2c will process up to three additional ones. Note that in spite of my dislike of multiple commands per line, I was perfectly happy to put three very simple commands on that line.

What now remains to have a useful product? This material must be entered into a file, with a final **x** command (otherwise the results of your labor will be lost!) at the end. If this file is called **change**, and your references (in NLM format) are in **biblio**, the command

    ex − biblio < change

will change all the references in **biblio** into our UNIX format. Figure 11–9 shows the final product. It is not the easiest thing in the world to understand, and takes some time to figure out, but it can save an enormous amount of work.

1	*g/^[0-9]/s/^/%Z /*
2′	*g/^AU/s/AU −/%A/ *
2a′	*s/$/./ *
2b′	*s/\([A−Z]\)\([A−Z]\.\)/ \1. \2/ *
2c′	*& | & | &*
3	*g/^TI/s/TI −/%T/*
4	*g/^SO/s/SO −/%J/ *
5	*a*
6	**
7′	*.*
8	*−s/ *19[0-9][0-9]/ *
9	*%D&/*
10	*g/^%D/s/ *[A-Za-z][^0-9]*/ *
11	*%V /*
12	*g/^%V/s/:/ *
13	*%P /*
14	**x**

Fig. 11–9: Full commands for bibliographic example.

NOTES TO CHAPTER 11

1. The output of compilers is made executable by the compiler.

2. I have taken the liberty of adding initials to the names of the last two authors.

3. Things get more complicated when you have to deal with things like *Proceedings of the 19.. conference on ....*

12

OTHER UNIX
EDITING TOOLS

The editors are obviously the main editing tool in any computing environment, and in many they may be the sole one. The UNIX system has a number of powerful editing tools, more or less closely related to the editors. All have pattern-matching capabilities; some use the **ex** patterns, others use a wider class of patterns, while one uses a more restricted class but works much faster.

This final chapter will mention the most important of these and give just enough detail to help you decide whether to pursue any one of them further. They are well described in the books by Bourne and by Kernighan and Pike (full references in App. F).

12.1 THE GREP FAMILY

One of the first tools many users learn about is the pattern finder, **grep**.[1] It is based on the same pattern finding mechanism as **ed** and **ex**. The command

    grep *pat filename*

will print out all lines in *filename* that contain *pat*. If the pattern consists entirely of numbers and letters it does not need to be put in quotation marks, but if it contains special characters it is advisable to do so. In almost all cases either single or double quotes will do. The simplest example (and the one most UNIX users use) is to develop an online telephone directory. If you have a file like the telephone numbers file used in Chap. 10 called **phone**, it is easy to find any person's phone number. The command

    grep Doe phone

should produce the output

    Doe, Jane   2-1234

Note that there is no need to sort the file or keep it in any order. If you have more than one Doe in the file, you will get them all, which rarely matters.

It is also useful if you find yourself using **vi** from an unfamiliar terminal and do not know what the system calls it. As noted in the Epilogue to Part II, file **/etc/termcap** contains the full names, the UNIX abbreviations, and the characteristics of the terminals the system knows. Using **grep** on that file can give you the abbreviation of your terminal. The following example shows you how to discover the system name for a Hazeltine 1500 terminal:

    grep '[Hh]azel' /etc/termcap

    H5|h1500|hazeltine 1500:
    H6|h1510|hazeltine 1510:
    H8|h1520|hazeltine 1520:
    H7|h2000|hazeltine 2000:

The first line is the command that you give; the next four show the computer's response. Note that if you do not know whether the first letter of the full name is in upper or lower case, you can use the character class notation.

Another use of **grep** on a single file is to extract records with a certain pattern. The UNIX spelling checker has a file called, on many systems, **/usr/dict/words**, which contains some 25,000 words. If you want the extract all eight letter words from it you could give the command

> grep '^........$' /usr/dict/words > eights

This will put all eight letter words into **eights**. Let me give you a challenge posed in Kernighan and Plaugher's Software Tool books (see App. F for full reference). They attribute the problem to D. E. Knuth (but give no reference). It is: Find the largest set of eight letter words with the same *middle* four letters. It requires the use of the **sort** and **uniq** programs. The solution is given at the end of this chapter.

If **grep** is used on several files simultaneously by giving the command

> **grep** *pat filelist*

where *filelist* is a list of files, it will print out all matching lines, prefacing each by the name of the file it is in. Thus if you have a whole lot of files named rather uninformatively *letter1*, *letter2*, and so on, and you want to find the one addressed to "Dear Bob," the command

> **grep 'Dear Bob:' lett***

will find you the file containing a letter that contains that pattern. Note that replacing the pattern "Dear Bob:" by the simpler "Bob" would also produce all references to Bob in letters written to others.

In addition to the widely used **grep** program there are two other similar ones that are much less well known. The first is **fgrep**, which stands for fast grep. It is a program that will allow for the simultaneous searching of a file for several strings of characters. It was developed in a bibliographic context to allow fast searching for several keywords simultaneously. Unlike most UNIX pattern matchers, this one can only search for explicitly given strings, without any metacharacters. In exchange, it is very fast.

The second program, called **egrep** (for extended grep), can search for patterns of greater generality than can the other programs. The patterns it can search for are technically known as **regular expressions**. The editors and **grep** can search for the commonest types of regular expressions (the patterns we can make with the metacharacters described in Chap. 10); **egrep** can search for regular expressions in their full generality, but it would take things too far afield to describe them here.

12.2 SED

This is a non–interactive stream editor that reads a file line by line from standard input, optionally modifies each line, and puts it out on standard output. Unlike the other editors it does not need to have the whole file potentially accessible all the time. This leads to its ability to edit files of essentially unlimited size on machines with limits on the size of the files they can manipulate. Furthermore, on machines with no such limitations, such as the VAX, it consumes far fewer resources.

To use **sed** you can either put the editing commands on the command line, or in a file much like the editor scripts discussed in Chap. 11. In the former case you must precede the editing commands, usually put in quotes, by a **−e** flag; in the latter the filename of the file containing the editor script should be preceded by a **−f** flag. You almost never want input to come from the keyboard, or output to go to the terminal, so both standard input and standard output are usually redirected.

In Chap. 11 I gave an example of using an editor script to use **ex** to change all occurrences of "CTRL" to "Control." It is clear that in this application each line is processed only once, and that you therefore have no need for the full power of the **ex** editor. To make the changes in a single file you would first rename it, (say **temp**) using the **mv** command, then give the command

    sed < temp > chap*n* −e 's/CTRL/Control/g'

Finally you would remove **temp**. Fig. 12–1 shows how the file of commands first given as Fig. 11–5 would be modified to use **sed** rather than **ex** to carry out the changes. At the bottom of the file you would add a single **rm temp** command.

mv app1 temp; sed < temp > app1 −e 's/CTRL/Control/g'
mv app2 temp; sed < temp > app2 −e 's/CTRL/Control/g'
mv app3 temp; sed < temp > app3 −e 's/CTRL/Control/g'
mv app4 temp; sed < temp > app4 −e 's/CTRL/Control/g'
mv chap0 temp; sed < temp > chap0 −e 's/CTRL/Control/g'

Fig. 12–1: Start of **mybook** file using **sed.**

In this case using **sed** would allow slightly cheaper computing, and for such infrequently used manipulations it may well be questioned whether the savings justify using a less familiar tool. On the other hand, **sed** is indisputably very useful when you need to change data from the format in which it is stored to that needed by a command.

As an example, consider a form-letter-processing system. One component is a mailing list entry and update system; the other is the letter-writing system. The former finds it convenient to store each address as a single line, with its fields separated by semicolons. My office address would be stored as

00el Lozy;01Mohamed;02665 Huntington Avenue;
03Boston;04MA;0502115

On the other hand, the letter-writing program needs it in the form shown in Fig. 12–2. The question arises: which program should be coerced into using the format of the other? The UNIX answer is simple: neither. A small program, called a **filter**, is interposed between the two, taking the output of the first and changing it into the input format needed by the second.

.ds 00 "el Lozy
.ds 01 "Mohamed
.ds 02 "665 Huntington Avenue
.ds 03 "Boston
.ds 04 "MA
.ds 05 "02115

Fig. 12–2: Address format for letter writing program.

12.2.1 Pipes and Filters

Most UNIX programs have the option of taking input from the standard input, and many will put their output on standard output unless directed to do otherwise. This allows programs to collaborate, with the output of one being used as the input of another. Let's begin with a classic example. How can you count the number of current users of the system? There is a command, **who,** which will put the names of the users together with some other information onto standard output, one user per line. You can redirect this output into a file, say **temp,** then count the number of lines in it with the **wc** command. Then you must remove the **temp** file. The sequence of commands is

```
who > temp
wc −1 temp
rm temp
```

This is a clumsy way of doing things, though it is often the best that can be done on a non–UNIX system. On UNIX you can send the standard output produced by one program to the standard input of another, using what is known as a **pipe.** The above sequence of three commands would be abbreviated to the single line

```
who | wc −1
```

where | is the pipe symbol.

The **sed** is very well suited to making pipes that transform data from one format to another. To return to our form-letter program, you can keep the data in the format required by the address maintenance program and then run it through **sed** to put it into the format required by the mailing program.

Since this is something that will be done fairly regularly, it is clearly worth while putting the editing commands into a file. Fig. 12–3 shows one sequence that will do what is needed. Study it to be sure that you understand it.

```
s/../.ds & "/
s/;\(..\)/ \
.ds \1 "/g
```

Figure 12–3: Commands for modification of mailing list file.

If these commands are in a file called **change** and the original addresses in a file called **address,** the command

> sed < address −f change | form

will take the address file, put each record in the format of Fig. 12–2, and deliver the reformatted data to **form,** which is the form-letter-generating program. The example was simplified to avoid cluttering up with details; it does show what **sed** can do. For more details on **sed** see the appropriate section of the Programmer's Guide, referred to in App. F., and the books cited at the start of this chapter.

12.3 AWK

This program presumably derives its unharmonious name from the last names of its three authors (see App. F for a full reference). It is a very powerful pattern-matching and file-modifying program, which in addition can do arithmetic calculations on the contents of the files it acts on.

It is impossible to even start to describe the full range of functions of this program. The one point I would like to note is that it makes extensive use of the concept of fields separated by tabs. It refers to the first field of a line as **$1**, the second as **$2**, and so on. If you have a table with five columns of entries separated by tabs, and you wish to interchange the second and third columns, all you need to enter is

> awk 'print [$1,$3,$2,$4,$5]' oldtab > newtab

where **oldtab** is assumed to be the name of the file containing the original table, and **newtab** that which will contain the modified one. As with **sed,** the commands (here often called program) may be on the command line or in a file; in the latter case the filename should be preceded by a −f flag.

awk is in fact a powerful programming language that is very suited for certain jobs. If at all interested, I urge you to read its full description.

12.4 OTHER EDITORS

The official UNIX editors are **ed** and **vi/ex**. You may find one or two other editors, especially if you are in a university environment. Before using them, check their status. They are likely to receive little support from the computing facility, and may well contain bugs.

The first of these is **teco**, a programmable, originally line-oriented editor. While it is not supported by UNIX systems, you may find a locally supported version which may well have had some screen-oriented features added. It may be worth your while to try it out if you are adventurous, but I doubt that you will prefer it to **vi/ex**.

The second, and more important, is **EMACS**, the self–documenting, customizable, extensible, real-time display editor. It was developed by Richard M. Stallman at the MIT Artificial Intelligence Laboratory, and for several years UNIX versions have been floating around the academic community. Many were of dubious parentage and reliability, with local modifications. Commercial versions now available should provide a more dependable environment.

EMACS is substantially larger than **vi**, and thus does not run on the smaller microcomputer adaptations of UNIX. While it has even more commands than **vi**, it is a modeless editor, i.e., entering a given key will always have the same effect. This gives it a very different "feel" from **vi**. If available, try it; you may well prefer it to **vi**.

12.5 ANSWER TO KNUTH'S CHALLENGE

Did you try to solve the problem of finding the largest set of words with the same middle four letters? Here is a solution. I assume that you know about **sort** and **uniq** (if not, why not learn about them?). The first step is to extract all eight letter words from **/usr/dict/words**, and as indicated above one way would be using **grep**:

```
grep '^........$' /usr/dict/words > eights
```

You will need the file **eights** later, so do not change it. First, however, you need a file of middle letters. Using either **sed** or **ex**, it is not difficult to replace each word (line) by its middle letters using the two commands

s/^../ / s/..$//

where the first substitution removes the first two characters, and the second the last two. However you do it, put the output in a file called **middle**. The command

sort middle −o middle

will sort that file, and put the sorted output back into it (the **−o** flag tells it where to put the output). The command

uniq −c middle count

will remove repeated lines and output one copy of each, preceded by the number of repetitions, putting the result into **count**. Finally

sort −nr count −o count

will sort the lines on the first numeric field in reverse order, i.e., the most frequent middle letters will be first.

On our system, the most frequent middle letters were "ippi," which occurred 11 times. To find the words in which they occurred, the command

grep '^..ippi' eights

was given, producing the list shown in Fig. 12–4.

chipping
clipping
dripping
flipping
gripping
quipping
shipping
skipping

slipping
tripping
whipping

Fig. 12–4: Answer to Knuth's challenge.

NOTES TO CHAPTER 12

1. The name **grep** comes from the **ed** command you would give to obtain the same result: **g/re/p**, a global command to print the lines containing a given regular expression.

Appendix A: Summary of vi Commands

The following commands are in effect while in text entry mode. In many cases, they depend on the setting of certain options.

Control–D	back up over one level of indentation if auto-indent set (6.4)
0Control–D	kill autoindent (6.4)
^Control–D	kill autoindent on this line, restore it on next (6.4)
Control–H	delete last input character (3.1)
Control–T	if in autoindent mode, insert one **shiftwidth** blank or tab (6.4)
Control–W	delete last input word (3.1)
ESC	return to command mode from insertion mode (2.1)
INT	interrupt insertion, return to command mode (2.1)
erase	delete last character entered (3.1)
kill	delete input on this line (3.1)

The following are the **vi** commands. They are listed with the following sequence: control characters, upper case letters, lower case letters, and finally all symbols, in ASCII collating sequence.

Control–B*	move backward one page (4.4.1)
Control–D	scroll down (4.4.1)
Control–E*	expose one more line at bottom of screen (4.4.1)
Control–F*	move forward one page (4.4.1)
Control–G	print statistics on current file and position (4.4.1)
Control–H	move back one space (**h** better) (4.4.1)
Control–J	move to corresponding position on next line (**j** better) (4.4.1)
Control–L	redraw screen, useful if scrambled (6.3.3)
Control–M	same as **CR** (4.4.1)
Control–N	move to corresponding position on next line (**j** better) (4.4.1)
Control–P	move to corresponding position on previous line (**k** better) (4.4.1)
Control–R	redraw screen, eliminating deleted lines marked by @ (6.3.3)
Control–U	scroll up (4.4.1)
Control–Y*	expose one more line at top of screen (4.4.1)
Control–Z*	suspend currently active UNIX command (8.2.4)
Control–]	same as **:ta** with word after cursor as argument (7.7)
Control– `	same as **vi** # (7.5)
A	append text at end of current line (3.2)
B	move to start of current big word (4.3.1)
CR	move to first non–blank position on next line (3.2)
C	change to end of line (5.1.3)
D	delete to end of line (5.1.3)

---

*This command is not present in all versions of the editor. Throughout this book, all commands (whether editor or UNIX) that may be absent, or function differently, on certain systems will be marked with an asterisk. These differences will be discussed in App. E.

E	move to end of current big word (4.3.1)
F*x*	move backward to character *x* on current line (4.3.3)
*n***G**	move to start of line *n* (4.4.1)
H	move to start of top line on current screen (4.4.1)
I	insert text at beginning of current line (3.2)
J	join next line to current one smartly (5.1.6)
L	move to start of last line on current screen (4.4.1)
M	move to start of middle line on current screen (4.4.1)
N	search for pattern in opposite direction (4.4.3)
O	insert line above current line (3.3)
P	put contents of a buffer into text before cursor (5.2)
R	replace characters by overtyping (5.1)
S	change line (5.1.3)
T*x*	move backward to character after *x* on current line (4.3.3)
U	undo all current changes on current line (5.2)
W	move to start of next big word (4.3.1)
X	delete character before cursor (5.1.1)
Y	copy current line into buffer (5.2)
ZZ	save file and quit (2.5)
a	append text (2.4)
b	move to start of current word (4.3.1)
c	change object (2.4)
d	delete object (2.4)
e	move to end of current word (4.3.1)
f*x*	move forward to character *x* on currentt line (4.3.3)
h	move left one space (2.3)
i	insert text (2.2)
j	move down one line (2.3)
k	move up one line (2.3)
l	move right one space (**space** is better) (2.3)
m*x*	associate a mark (*x*) with current position of cursor (4.4.1)

n	search for pattern in same direction (4.4.3)
o	insert line below current line (3.3)
p	put contents of a buffer into text after cursor (5.2)
r	replace character (2.4)
s	change characters (5.1.1)
t*x*	move forward to character before *x* on current line (4.3.3)
u	undo last change (2.4)
w	move to start of next word (4.3.1)
x	remove character (2.4)
y	copy object into buffer (5.2)
z	redraw screen around current line (6.3.3)
space	move right one space (2.3)
-	move to first non–blank position on previous line (3.2)
!*object command*	send lines from current line to *object* to *command*, and replace them by its output (8.2.1)
$	move to end of current line (4.3.2)
%	if given with cursor on (, { or [, moves it to matching), } or] (6.4)
"	return to start of line you were previously on (4.4.1)
'*x*	move to start of line containing mark *x* (4.4.1)
(	move to start of current sentence (4.4.2)
)	move to start of next sentence (4.4.2)
+	move cursor to first non–blank character on next line (**CR** better) (4.4.1)
-	move cursor to first non–blank character on previous line (4.4.1)
.	repeat last command which changed buffer (5.1.6)
/*pat***CR**	move forward to first occurrence of pattern *pat* (4.4.3)
0	move to start of current line (4.3.2)
<	decrease indent of each level of object by one shiftwidth (6.4)

=*	reindent lisp program, as if it had been entered using lisp and autoindent options (6.4)
>	indent each line of object by one more shiftwidth (6.4)
?*pat*CR	move backward to first occurrence of pattern *pat* (4.4.3)
[[	move to start of current section (4.4.2)
n|	move to column *n* on current line (4.3.2)
]]	move to start of next section (4.4.2)
^	move to first non–blank character on current line (4.3.2)
`*x*	go to position marked *x* (4.4.1)
``	return to previous position (4.4.1)
{	move to start of current paragraph (4.4.2)
}	move to start of next paragraph (4.4.2)
~*	change case of character if alphabetic (5.1.1)

Appendix B: Summary of ex Commands

Control–D	scroll down one window (9.4.3)
ab * *lhs rhs*	whenever *lhs* occurs in input as a word, replace it by *rhs* (8.3.1)
append	(abbr: **a**) append text after address (9.4.1)
arg	list files being edited (7.6)
change	(abbr: **c**) delete text addressed and replace by following (9.4.1)
copy	(abbr: **co**) copy addressed lines to after third address (9.4.2)
delete	(abbr: **d**) delete addressed text (9.4.1)
f *filename*	associate *filename* with contents of buffer (7.3.1)

---

*This command is not present in all versions of the editor. Throughout this book, all commands (whether editor or UNIX) that may be absent, or function differently, on certain systems will be marked with an asterisk. These differences will be discussed in Appendix E.

f	show summary statistics of file (same as Control-G) (7.3.1)
*n1, n2***g/***pat***/***command*	find lines between *n1* and *n2* which contain *pat*, then do *command* on each (8.1.4)
insert	(abbr: **i**) insert text before address (9.4.1)
j	join lines smartly (9.4.6)
list	(abbr: l) print lines more unambiguously on terminal (9.4.3)
map* *lhs rhs*	replace *lhs* by *rhs* in command mode (8.3.2)
map!* *lhs rhs*	whenever *lhs* occurs in input, replace by *rhs* (8.3.1)
map!*	list macros currently defined (8.3.1)
map*	list currently active macros (8.3.2)
move	(abbr: **m**) move addressed lines to after third address (9.4.2)
n *filelist*	edit *filelist* (7.6)
n!	edit next file, discarding changes in current buffer (7.6)
n	edit next file in argument list (7.6)
number	(abbr: **nu** or **#**) print lines on terminal (9.4.3)
preserve	save buffer as if system had crashed (9.4.6)
print	(abbr: **p**) print lines on terminal (9.4.3)
put	(abbr: **pu**) copy lines from buffer into file (9.4.2)
q!	quit editor without saving changes (2.5)
q	quit editor (2.5)
r *filename*	read *filename* into buffer below current line (7.3.2)
*n***r** **!***command*	execute *command* and place input in buffer after line *n* (8.2.3)
recover	recover file from save area (9.4.6)
rew	rewind argument list (7.6)
s/*pat***/***repl*	replace first occurrence of *pat* by *repl* on current line (8.1.3)

shell	spawn a new shell (9.4.6)
source	(abbr: **so**) read a file and execute instructions in it (9.4.6)
stop*	suspend editor command (9.4.6)
stop!*	suspend editor command discarding changes in current buffer (9.4.6)
ta* *function*	move to defining line of *function* (7.7)
ta!* *function*	move to defining line of *function* discarding changes in buffer (7.7)
transpose	(abbr: **t**) same as copy (which is preferable) (9.4.2)
unmap* *lhs*	remove *lhs* from list of macros (8.3.2)
unmap!* *lhs*	remove *lhs* from list of macros (8.3.1)
vi #	read alternate file into buffer and edit in visual mode (7.5)
vi *filename*	read *filename* into buffer and edit it in visual mode (7.5)
vi! *filename*	read *filename* into buffer and edit it in visual mode discarding changes in current buffer (7.5)
w	write buffer to file it came from (7.3.1)
w *filename*	write buffer to *filename* (7.3.1)
w > > *filename*	append contents of the buffer to the end of *filename* (7.3.1)
w!	write buffer if system allows, overriding editor constraints (7.8)
yank	(abbr: **y**) copy addressed lines into buffer (9.4.2)
z	print a window of text in the appropriate format (9.4.3)
!*command*	spawn new shell to execute *command*, return to editor (8.2.2)
=	print number of addressed line (**$** default) (9.4.3)

Appendix C: Summary of Options

autoindent	(ai, noai) set autoindentation feature (6.4)
autoprint	(ap, ap) print result after most commands (9.2.5)
autowrite	(aw, noaw) automatically write out buffer (if changed) before **:n**, **:rew**, **:stop**, **:ta**, or **:!** commands given in visual mode (7.9.1)
beautify	(bf, nobf) prevent entry of control characters (6.6)
ignorecase	(ic, noic) ignore distinction between upper and lower case in searches (8.1.2)
lisp	(lisp, lisp) autoindent indents appropriately for lisp, and (), {}, and [] commands suitably redefined (6.4)
list	(list, nolist) print lines more unambiguously (9.4.3)

magic	(magic, magic) metacharacters have their normal significance (8.1.2)
mesg	(mesg, mesg) allow messages to be received (6.3.3)
number	(nu, nonu) automatically number lines (9.4.3)
optimize	(opt, noopt) abolishes automatic **CR** when terminal prints (6.3.3)
paragraphs = *xxxx*	(para, para = IPLPPPQPP Llbp) specifies paragraph macros used by { and } commands (6.5)
prompt	(prompt, prompt) set prompt in **ex** (9.0)
redraw	(redraw, noredraw) simulate intelligent terminal on dumb one (6.3.3)
scroll = *xx*	(scroll, scroll = ½ window) set scrolling parameter to *xx* lines (**ex** only) (6.3.2)
sections = *xxxx*	(sections, sections = SHNHH HU) specifies section macros used by [[and]] commands (6.5)
shiftwidth = *xx*	(sw, sw = 8) number of characters to be backspaced over by Control–D when autoindent is on (6.4)
showmatch	(sm, nosm) when (or { is entered, move cursor for one second to matching) or } (6.4)
slowopen	(slow, terminal dependent) delays updating of screen during insertions (6.3.3)
tabstop = *xx*	(ts, ts = 8) set editor tabs every *xx* characters (6.4)
taglength = *x*	(tl, tl=0) only first *x* characters of tag are significant (7.7)
tags = *path of files*	(tags, tags = tags/usr/lib/tags) path of files to be searched for tags (7.7)
w300 = *xx*	set window size to *xx* lines if speed is 300 baud (6.3.1)
window = *xx*	(window, speed dependent) set window size to *xx* lines (6.3.1)

wrapmargin $= xx$ (wm, wm $= 0$) set margin for word wraparound at xx characters from end of line (6.5)

writeany   (wa, nowa) allow user to write to any file the system allows him to (7.9.2)

wrapscan   (ws, ws) searches will wrap around past end of file (8.1.2)

Appendix D:
The ex/vi
Command Line

As noted in the text, both **ex** and **vi** are normally invoked by simply giving the command followed by the name of the file (less commonly, files) to be edited. Most of the command line arguments are rarely used; they are given here for reference. Unless the contrary is explicitly stated, all options apply to both editors.

–	This applies only to **ex** and suppresses the interactive dialogue. Its only use is in editor scripts in command files (Sec. 11.2).
−**v**	This again only applies to the **ex** editor, and makes it come up in visual mode. It is therefore equivalent to the **vi** command.
−**t** *tag*	This is equivalent to giving a **tag** command immediately after entering the editor. It will edit the appropriate file and position the editor at the defining position. It obviously needs a suitable **tags** file (Sec. 7.7). There is no need to give a filename when using this flag.

−**r**	This is used to retrieve a file lost due to a system crash or disconnected line. Given with a filename it will retrieve that file; otherwise it will give a list of saved files.
−**l**	This sets the editor up for editing lisp programs, turning the **showmatch** and **lisp** options on.
−**x**	This sets the editor up to process encrypted files (Sec. 7.10).
−**w** *n*	This will set the editor up with a window size of *n*, useful if you wish to override the default or the value set in your **.exrc** file without giving a **se window** command from the editor.
−**R**	This sets the editor in the read only mode. In **vi** it may be more convenient to use the **view** command, which invokes **vi** in that mode (Sec. 7.8).
+*command*	This is most often used to get the editor to start the session at a given position. If + is followed by an address of any kind, the editor will be positioned at that address, otherwise it will be at the last line.
	Finally after some or all of these flags, comes the name of the file or files being edited.

Appendix E:
Editor Versions

This book describes version 3.6 of the editor running under the Berkeley 4.2 release of UNIX. Almost everything in it will apply to any system that supports the editor, the very few exceptions having been noted with asterisks in the text. In this appendix, what is likely to be found under different versions and how much the differences matter will be discussed.

E.1 UNIX VERSIONS

Many microcomputer implementations of UNIX claim to be a given Bell Laboratories version "with Berkeley enhancements." The latter almost always include the **vi/ex** editor and some version of the C shell, often without the **Control–Z** feature (Sec. 8.2.4). Such systems will not support the **ex** command **stop** (Sec. 9.4.5) either.

Most often, few of the many other Berkeley features are

present. Specifically, the **fmt**, **ctags**, **tset**, and **error** programs, together with the **sdb** and **dbx** debuggers, are absent on many microcomputer installations.

The editor features that may be absent depend on the basic version implemented. Many microcomputer implementations, including the **VENIX**[1] implementation that we use, have version 2.13 of the editor. They have, however, introduced some version 3 improvements into their version.

E.2 FEATURES ABSENT IN ALL VERSION 2 SYSTEMS

There are two sets of commands that may be missing in a given implementation. Some commands were only introduced in version 3, and so will be absent on all version 2 implementations. Others were present in version 2, but not supported on all implementations.

The most important set of commands not found in version 2 are the abbreviation and macro facilities. They are totally absent in version 2, and evolved in early releases of version 3. Early version 3 editors only supported **map**; **map!** was introduced with version 3.3 and **ab** with version 3.4.

Much less important is the absence of the **Control–E** and **Control–Y** commands. Finally, it is not at all clear when the ~ command was introduced, as even the version 3.5 manual does not mention it, though it is there!

A few features present in some or all implementations of version 2 have been modified in version 3. The most important is the **wrapmargin** option, which is much improved starting with version 3.4. The page moving commands, **Control–F** and **Control–B**, have been modified. In version 2, if preceded by a number, the window size is reset to that number, while in version 3 it tells the editor how many pages to move.

E.3 FEATURES ABSENT IN SOME VERSION 2 SYSTEMS

Finally, there are some features that are found in some, but not all, implementations of version 2. The page motions (**Control–F** and

Control–B) are absent in some implementations, and the **wrap-margin** option is also completely absent in some implementations.

On the programming front, **tags** and related commands and options are also absent in some implementations of version 2. Note that these commands are not very useful without the **ctags** program, a Berkeley product often absent on systems that claim to have "Berkeley enhancements." The **lisp** option and the = command are also absent in some version 2 editors. This does not matter much, as such machines are unlikely to support lisp.

E.4 THE VENIX IMPLEMENTATION FOR THE IBM PC/XT

As noted above, the VENIX implementation is based on version 2.13. It has, however, a few enhancements borrowed from version 3. Note that the manual does not describe all these additions. A good general rule when using a microcomputer implementation would be to try any feature that interests you, even if the manual does not mention it.

Almost all Berkeley features of UNIX are absent, apart from the editor, the termcap capability, and a primitive C shell that does not support **Control–Z**. None of the programs mentioned in the third paragraph of this appendix are present. I have found it worthwhile to develop a simple **fmt** program myself for use on the VENIX system; the other more complex programs I do without.

The editor has the version 3 form of the **Control–F** and **Control–B** commands. It also has the version 2 form of **wrap-margin**, which sometimes gets pretty confused. It has neither **tags** nor any of the abbreviation and macro capabilities. Everything else is there in some form.

I found it very unpleasant for text entry until I made my own version of **fmt**. It still does not do **wrapmargin** always the way it should, but now it is easy to correct overlong lines. Apart from its slowness on large files it is satisfactory, even if it does have a slightly different "feel" from the full version I use on the VAX.

Program entry in itself works perfectly, as all I need is the **auto-indent** option, which works well. I do not find the system really satisfactory for developing large programs. This is only partly due to the lack of the **tags** facility. The main reason has nothing to do with the editor, but rather with the lack of any symbolic debugger.

All in all, I find this a very good approximation to the true **vi** editor which I use on the VAX. Indeed, I am very pleased with the entire system, which gives a very large part of UNIX on a very modest machine.

NOTES FOR APPENDIX E

1. VENIX is a trademark of VenturCom Inc.

Appendix F:
Further Reading

You may wish to read more about the topics explicitly dealt with in this book, or about the UNIX system in general. The suggested readings are given under the followng headings:

1. Documentation on the use of the UNIX programs described in this book.
2. More general material on editors and editing.
3. Material on the UNIX system.

F.1 DOCUMENTATION OF PROGRAMS DESCRIBED

The primary source of information for the **ex** and **vi** editors are two documents included in the *UNIX Programmer's Manual:*

1. "An Introduction to Display Editing With **vi**," by William Joy, revised for versions 3.5/2.13 by Mark Horton.

2. **"Ex** Reference Manual Version 3.5/2.13," by William Joy, revised for versions 3.5/2.13 by Mark Horton.

These two papers are hard reading for the uninitiated; indeed, that is why this book was written. Once this book has been read, however, serious users will want the official documentation. While this book is almost complete, I have omitted some of the more uninteresting options, commands, and special cases.

The *UNIX Programmer's Manual* contains three tutorial articles on editing; unfortunately all three deal with line editing. They are:

3. "Edit: A Tutorial," by Ricki Blau and James Joyce. **Edit** is a subset of **ex**, which allows neither operation in the screen mode nor metacharacters. This paper is a very slow paced introduction; it may irritate many readers but may well be just what the gun–shy need.

4. "A Tutorial Introduction to the UNIX Text Editor," by Brian W. Kernighan. Like all of Dr. Kernighan's writings, this is a model of lucidity, giving a gentle introduction to line-oriented editing with **ed**. Like the previous paper, it may be of use to readers who, for some reason, have to use the line-oriented editor.

5. "Advanced Editing on UNIX," by Brian W. Kernighan. This is essential reading for anyone making substantial systematic changes to structured files using a line-oriented editor. While much of the material in it has been covered in Chapters 9 to 11 of this book, any serious user of the editor should read this paper.

Finally, there are the two programs, **sed** and **awk**. The description of both in Chap. 12 is very brief; the interested reader will have to study the original descriptions. Both are described in the *UNIX Programmer's Manual*:

6. SED–A Non-Interactive Text Editor, by Lee E. McMahon. Carefully note the author's warning:

Because of the differences between interactive and non–interactive operation, considerable changes have been made between **ed** and **sed**; even confirmed users of **ed** will frequently be surprised (and probably chagrined) if they rashly use **sed** without reading Sections 2 and 3 of this document.

You have been warned, and the warning is appropriate.

7. Awk - A Pattern Scanning and Processing Language (second edition), by Alfred V. Aho, Brian W. Kernighan, and Peter J. Weinberger.

F.2 MATERIAL ABOUT EDITORS

Three good surveys about editors have been published, all in publications available from the Association for Computing Machinery, 1133 Avenue of the Americas, New York, NY 10036. They are:

1. "On–line Text Editing: A Survey," by Andreas Van Dam and D. E. Rice, *ACM Computing Surveys* 3(3), 1971. The best introduction to the history (prehistory?) of editors.

2. Proceedings of the Sigplan Sigoa Symposium on text manipulation (Portland, Oregon, 1981) are published as the June 1981 issue of the *ACM SIGPLAN NOTICES*. These proceedings give an excellent overview of what is being done in the field of sophisticated editing now. Many of the products described are not yet in general use, but probably some will soon be.

3. "On–line Text Editing: A Survey, Parts I and II," by Norman Meyrowitz and Andries Van Dam, *Computing Surveys*, 14:321-352 and 353-415, 1982. An update on the earlier survey, very detailed (almost 100 pages). Part I is a general introduction to the field of current editors, defining terms and introducing issues. Part II presents a large number of editors, illustrating the various capabilities described in Part I.

There is no point in trying to keep track of the innumerable papers dealing with editors and editing. I will, however, mention one recent paper: "The Evalution of Computer Text Editors: Methodology and Empirical Results," by Teresa L. Roberts and Thomas P. Moran, *Communications of the ACM*, 26:265-283, 1983.

As the title indicates, the article begins by defining a methodology for the evaluation of editors, and applies it to several rather different editors.

F.2.1 THEORY OF PATTERN MATCHING

Pattern matching is an important part of computer science, with many applications other than editing. Two frequently cited treatments of it are:

1. *The Theory of Parsing, Translation and Compiling, Volume I: Parsing* by Alfred V. Aho and Jeffrey D. Ullman, Englewood Cliffs, NJ: Prentice-Hall, Inc., 1972.

2. *The Design and Analysis of Computer Algorithms* by Alfred V. Aho, John E. Hopcroft, and Jeffrey D. Ullman, Reading, MA: Addison-Wesley Publishing Company, 1974.

Both of these books are very mathematical and do not deal with the practical aspects of designing a program to match patterns. A more accessible introduction is given in:

3. *Principles of Compiler Design* by Alfred V. Aho and Jeffrey D. Ullman, Reading, MA: Addison-Wesley Publishing Company, 1974. This is less theoretical and does discuss the general approach to designing pattern matching programs, but few specifics.

4. *Algorithms* by Robert Sedgewick, Reading, MA: Addison-Wesley Publishing Company, 1983. Chapters 19 to 21 of this very readable book give an excellent introduction to the whole subject of pattern matching.

Finally, Chap. 6 of either version of the Software Tools book (Sec. F.3.2) has an excellent discussion of how to write a program that will match most of the kinds of patterns that **ex** matches.

F.3 MATERIAL ABOUT THE UNIX SYSTEM

There are two groups of publications that come under this heading: guides on how to use the UNIX system and works describing its philosophy and organization.

F.3.1 GUIDES TO THE UNIX SYSTEM

The authoritative source of information about the UNIX system is the *UNIX Programmer's Manual,* available from your installation.[1] Part I of it is available on–line using the **man** command. To find out how to use it, just enter

man man

You may well find that the *Programmer's Manual* is too extensive (and expensive!) for your needs. In that case, you can usually obtain copies of individual sections. Beginners should definitely get a copy of

1. "UNIX for Beginners" (second edition) by Brian W. Kernighan. This is a first-rate introduction to using UNIX for either programming or document preparation.

   Sooner or later you will need to use the facilities of the UNIX shell. There are two widely available shells on UNIX systems; the standard Bourne shell is documented in

2. "An Introduction to the UNIX Shell" by S. R. Bourne, while the Berkeley C Shell is documented in

3. "An Introduction to the C Shell" by William Joy.

The justified popularity of UNIX (and the dismal documentation that accompanies it) have led to the publication of many books describing the system. I cannot review all the books published over the last few years, but will describe my favorite books for readers in three categories: beginning, intermediate, and advanced. For the absolute beginner who is afraid of computers, the best book by far is

1. *A UNIX Primer* by Ann Nichols Lomuto and Nico Lomuto, Englewood Cliffs, NJ:Prentice-Hall, Inc., 1983. This is an excellent book for the gun-shy, illustrating the essentials of the UNIX system through text processing applications. It describes the use of the **ed** editor and **nroff** text formatter to produce documents, and in the process gives an over-

view of the fundamentals of the UNIX system. It covers the elementary material as well, but does not go very far, and its style will irritate those readers who do not want to be spoonfed.

At the intermediate level, one book stands out both for its writing and its content:

2. *Introducing the UNIX System* by Henry McGilton and Rachel Morgan, New York, McGraw-Hill Company, 1983. This is a book that is truly useful for both the beginner and the more experienced user. It is written in a style suitable for the beginner, but covers a lot of material that most elementary books leave out. It discusses both the **ed** and **vi** editors at length, as well as the **sed**, **grep** family, and **awk** programs. It has a good discussion of formatting, including the Berkeley **me** macros, the **csh** in particular, and the Berkeley enhancements in general. Finally, it has a reasonable section on the system manager's programming tools.

Finally, there are two books that, whatever their authors may claim, are advanced books for the advanced user interested in programming. Both share the view that the shell and the pattern matching utilties are really programming tools in their own right. Finally, both are written by distinguished members of the Bell Laboratories group that developed UNIX. For the advanced user there is no question which to get: both!

3. *The UNIX System* by S. R. Bourne, Reading, MA: Addison-Wesley Publishing Company, 1982. While the preface claims that "...all users from the novice to the expert should find it useful," it is clearly aimed at the more experienced user. For such a user it will prove invaluable; I learned a couple of things browsing through it in the bookstore, and keep finding useful points. While all the book is excellent, I will single out the section on document preparation for special mention. The author actually gives the macros he used to typeset the book. Studying them will expose the reader to advanced formatting in a way nothing else will.

4. *The UNIX Programming Environment* by Brian W. Ker-

nighan and Rob Pike, Englewood Cliffs, New Jersey: Prentice-Hall, Inc., 1984. A book clearly aimed at programmers, and clearly any person programming in a UNIX environment should have it. There is little more to add except that it very clearly makes the point that the pattern matching programs and the shell are full–fledged programming languages.

F.3.2 READINGS ABOUT UNIX

There are two publications that give an excellent overview of the UNIX philosophy:

1. A special issue of the *Bell System Technical Journal* appearing as Part 2 of the July-August 1978 issue (Vol. 57 No. 2) devoted to the UNIX Time-Sharing System.[2] It contains about twenty articles on different aspects of the UNIX system by those who developed it. The articles cover all aspects of its use and most readers will find several that interest them. Note that while general principles are of lasting value, specific details are of more ephemeral interest, and in the world of computers, 1978 was a long time ago!

2. *Software Tools* by Brian Kernighan and P. J. Plaugher, Reading, MA: Addison-Wesley Publishing Company, 1976. This is a unique book that describes the basic tools available in the UNIX system and gives programs to implement simplified versions of them. If you are interested in how an editor like **ed** works, Chapters 5 and 6 will show you. The programs in the original book are written in **ratfor**, a rational pre-processor for FORTRAN. A new version, with programs written in Pascal, is available: *Software Tools in Pascal* by Brian W. Kernighan and P. J. Plaugher, Reading, MA: Addison-Wesley Publishing Company, 1981.

Magazine articles on UNIX are proliferating in general computer publications, and there is no point in trying to keep track of them. I do want to note a pair of consecutive issues of *Byte*[3] magazine (August and September 1983) devoted respectively to the C language and UNIX on microcomputers.

In addition, specialized magazines dealing exclusively with UNIX have recently begun publication. Two of the earliest are *UNIX Review*, 2711 76th Avenue Southeast, Mercer Island, WA 98040 and *UNIX/WORLD*, P. O. Box 1165, Dover, NJ 07801.

NOTES FOR APPENDIX F

1. The Version 7 documentation is also available as a trade book published in two volumes by Holt, Rinehart, and Winston.

2. It is available from *The Bell System Technical Journal*, Bell Laboratories, Room 1J-319, J. F. Kennedy Parkway, Short Hills, NJ 07078.

3. Available from *Byte*, 70 Main Street, Peterborough, NH 03458.

Index